LEGENDS OF WARFARE

AVIATION

B-52 Stratofortress

Boeing's Iconic Bomber from 1952 to the Present

DAVID DOYLE

Schiffer Publishing Ltd

4880 Lower Valley Road • Atglen, PA 19310

Designed by Justin Watkinson
Type set in Impact/Minion Pro/Univers LT Std

ISBN: 978-0-7643-5587-5
Printed in China

Published by Schiffer Publishing, Ltd.
4880 Lower Valley Road
Atglen, PA 19310
Phone: (610) 593-1777; Fax: (610) 593-2002
E-mail: Info@schifferbooks.com
www.schifferbooks.com

Acknowledgments

I have been blessed with the generous help of many friends and
colleagues when preparing this manuscript. Truly, this book would
not have been possible without their collective assistance. Tom
Kailbourn; Scott Taylor; Dana Bell; and Brett Stolle at the National
Museum of the United States Air Force all gave of their time
without hesitation. My lovely and dear wife, Denise, has extended
help in countless ways and on countless occasions, not the least
of which are scanning photos, proofreading manuscripts, and
tending to the myriad of details of running the household without
much help from me. She has been my cheerleader throughout the
difficult parts of this project, and without her unflagging support
this could not have been completed.

Contents

Introduction

Boeing began producing aircraft before World War I, and by the 1930s was widely recognized as a cutting-edge innovator in aeronautics and aircraft design and manufacturing. Although Boeing was a prolific manufacturer of excellent fighter planes in the 1930s, during that decade the company began to produce the bombers for which it would become principally known. In 1934, the company invested $250,000 in a bomber design that in World War II would reap the firm, and America, huge dividends: the Model 299, which would evolve into the B-17. Seen here is the Y1B-17A (Boeing Model 299F), a special flight-test airplane powered by four Wright GR-1820-51 (G5) Cyclone engines with Moss/ General Electric turbosuperchargers. *National Museum of the United States Air Force*

While in the years leading up to the US involvement in World War II, the US Army Air Corps had experimented with very large, long-range bombers, in the form of the Boeing XB-15 and Douglas XB-19, it was Adolf Hitler's aggression that truly brought development of intercontinental bombers to the forefront.

In 1941, when the possibility of German forces overrunning all of Europe, including England, seemed all too real, serious effort began to be put into developing heavy bomber aircraft capable of striking Europe from bases in the United States. Two aircraft were borne from these efforts, the Northrop XB-35 Flying Wing, and the Consolidated B-36. Both types were originally designed to meet the requirement for a heavy bomber that could strike back at Hitler from the mainland US, but neither flew until the year after the German madman's death.

Although the B-36 was placed into production, World War II had also ushered in the jet age, and the military desired a bomber that could take advantage of the high speed potential demonstrated by the new powerplant. Work on the nation's first jet bomber had begun with design studies commissioned in 1943, and by 1944 specifications had been drawn up calling for a medium bomber with a 500 mph top speed.

This initial effort resulted in two production aircraft, the North American B-45 Tornado, which saw combat in Korea, and the Boeing B-47, which laid the cornerstone for the B-52. While the B-45 was essentially a conventional bomber design featuring jet engines, the B-47 had thin, swept wings with engines housed in underwing pods and bicycle landing gear. Pre-flight performance estimates, typically overoptimistic, were in many cases exceeded by the B-47 in flight.

In 1946, concurrent with the development of the B-47, Boeing was also contracted to produce an upgraded version of the famed B-29. Dubbed the B-50, the new aircraft was originally designated the B-29D, but was renumbered by the Air Force in part to present a more progressive image. More significant, in regards to this volume, was the drafting of requirements for a proposed second-generation intercontinental bomber to replace the B-36, which only then was taking to the air.

Along with Consolidated B-24 Liberators, Boeing B-17 Flying Fortresses carried out an effective strategic bombing campaign against Nazi Germany in World War II, greatly contributing to the Allied victory in Europe. Here, two B-17Gs, including Boeing-built B-17G-65-BO, serial number 43-37625, to the left, from the 323rd Bomb Squadron, 91st Bomb Group, 8th Air Force, fly high above the clouds during a mission. As part of the B-17 production pool, Douglas and Lockheed-Vega also built B-17Gs. *National Archives*

During World War II, the United States envisioned a need for a new type of long-range strategic bomber capable of flying missions across the Atlantic to Europe and returning to bases in North America. The Convair B-36 Peacemaker was produced to meet that requirement. It was the heaviest piston-engined aircraft ever made and was capable of delivering nuclear weapons at a combat radius of almost 4,000 miles. However, once the Soviet MiG jet fighters began to enter service, the B-36 was rendered obsolete as a nuclear-strike aircraft.

The Boeing B-47 Stratojet long-range, high-altitude strategic bomber entered service with the US Air Force's Strategic Air Command in 1951, roughly midway between the 1948 operational debut of the B-36 and the 1955 introduction of the Boeing B-52. Powered by six General Electric J-47 engines and featuring swept wings and tail, the B-47 had a combat radius of 2,013 miles, about half of that of the B-36, and could carry a bomb load of 25,000 pounds, as opposed to a normal bomb load of 72,000 pounds for the B-36, but the B-47 had a maximum speed of 607 miles per hour: 172 miles per hour faster than the B-36. The crew of the B-47 consisted of the pilot and the copilot, housed in tandem under a bubble canopy, and the navigator/bombardier, stationed in the nose. *National Archives*

Also roughly coinciding with the operational career of the Boeing B-47, and eventually replaced by that plane in the Strategic Air Command, was the Boeing B-50 Superfortress. This was an improved version of the B-29 Superfortress, featuring four powerful Pratt & Whitney R-4360 Wasp Major 28-cylinder radial piston engines. The B-50s were capable of carrying out nuclear-strike missions, and after they were retired from that role, many of them had second careers as tanker aircraft. *National Archives*

In the foreground is a Convair YB-60, a prototype strategic bomber which the Air Force considered, along with the B-52 and several other aircraft, for a strategic bomber in 1950. The YB-60 was achieved by mating several new components onto a Convair B-36 airframe, including a new, pointed nose; swept wings with eight pod-mounted Pratt & Whitney J57-P-3 turbojet engines; and a swept tail. Tests proved that the YB-60 was about one hundred miles per hour slower than the YB-52, the service-test version of the B-52, and, because of other deficiencies, the Air Force did not pursue the YB-60.
National Museum of the United States Air Force

CHAPTER 1
XB-52

Initially, the US Air Force issued an order to Boeing for two prototype XB-52s, but one of the two planes was redesignated the YB-52. The sole XB-52, serial number 49-230, was rolled out on November 29, 1951. Similar to the B-47, the XB-52 had a bubble canopy under which the pilot and the copilot sat in tandem. In this photo, they are visible, wearing flight helmets, seated in the cockpit. In addition, the crew included a navigator and a radar operator below the cockpit, and a tail gunner in the rear of the fuselage. There were two separate radomes: the upper one is matte black, and the lower one has a reddish-brown color. *National Archives*

When Boeing began work on a successor for the B-36, even though the prototype of that aircraft was just being completed by Consolidated, the desire of the military was to have a 450-mph capable intercontinental bomber capable of carrying 10,000 pounds of bombs 10,000 miles. Boeing's initial design under this 1946 study contract, the Model 462, was to achieve this by mounting six Wright T35 turboprop engines on a straight-wing airframe that very much resembled an enlarged B-29. The T35, under development since 1944, was expected to develop 5,500 horsepower. The company was to produce one mockup and two flying examples of the new aircraft, designated B-52, by early 1951.

However, development of the turboprop powerplant did not go smoothly, particularly in regard to marrying a propeller to the engine. Further, the design offered little improvement over the performance promised in the B-36. As a result, at a meeting at Wright Field, Dayton, Ohio, in October 1948, Col. Henry Edward "Pete" Warden suggested to the team of Boeing engineers there to discuss their new bomber program that Boeing consider using a pure jet, rather than turboprop engine.

Fortunately, a number of key engineers from Boeing happened to be in Dayton at that time. On Friday, October 22, 1948, a hastily assembled engineering group convened at the Hotel Van Cleve, where the Boeing men were staying.

George Schairer, Boeing chief of Aerodynamics, was joined by Edward C. Wells, Boeing vice president of engineering, and engineers Art Carlsen, Vaughn Blumenthal, Bob Withington, and

Maynard Pennell, and the men set out to redesign the B-52. By Friday night the men had laid out an eight-engine, swept-wing bomber. A Saturday morning visit to a local hobby shop brought back the materials to construct a presentation model of the new design, the Boeing Model 464. Ed Wells set out to produce design drawings, and on Sunday a stenographer was hired to type up the thirty-three-page proposal for the new aircraft. On Monday morning the proposal, drawings, and model were presented to Col. Warden, who was the Chief of Bombardment Branch, Engineering Division, USAF.

Warden was enthusiastic in his reception of the new design, and on January 26, 1949, the XB-52 was modified from the straight-wing, turboprop 464-17 to the swept-wing, 8-jet powered Model 464-49. On April 29, 1949, a full-size mockup of the revised B-52, which utilized at that time a two-seat inline canopy for the pilot and copilot, as did the B-47, was available for inspection by Air Force personnel.

With the mockup approved, work on the two flyable prototypes proceeded at a brisk pace, with the tarpaulin-swaddled XB-52 rolling out of Boeing's Seattle plant on November 29, 1951. While the XB-52 was the first of the new bombers to be completed, it was damaged by an explosion in the aircraft's pneumatic system during ground tests, and as a result, the YB-52 became the first of the type to take towards the air. The XB-52 did not fly until October 2, 1952.

During the official rollout of the XB-52 at Boeing's Seattle plant during the night of November 29, 1951, the aircraft is covered with white tarpaulins, to hide the aircraft from potential spies at or near the site. The view is from the rear, the vertical stabilizer and rudder assembly was folded down to the right, to allow clearance through the big door of the assembly building, and the shape of that assembly is visible under the tarpaulin. *National Museum of the United States Air Force*

The XB-52 is parked on a tarmac at Boeing Field in Seattle, in a photograph bearing the date of May 25, 1954, but possibly taken earlier. The prototype underwent a series of ground tests after its rollout, during which an explosion in the hydraulic system in one of the wings delayed the plane's first flight. The XB-52 finally had its maiden flight on October 2, 1952, more than six months after the initial flight of the YB-52. *National Archives*

The tail of Consolidated RB-36D-1-CF Peacemaker, serial number 44-92088, looms in the foreground of this photograph of the XB-52. The access doors on the bottom of the nacelles containing the four left Pratt & Whitney YJ57-P-3 turbojet engines are open. *National Museum of the United States Air Force*

As photographed from underneath the right wing of Consolidated B-36D-1-CF Peacemaker, serial number 44-92095, in the background are another B-36 (left) and the XB-52 (right). As in the preceding photograph, the access doors on the bottoms of the engine nacelles are open. *National Museum of the United States Air Force*

The XB-52 is viewed from the rear following a test flight. Trailing from the rear of the fuselage is the drag chute, which failed to fully deploy upon landing. A mockup of a tail turret was installed on the plane; faintly visible are the lines of the canopy for the tail gunner and, below it, the shape of the tail turret, with a radome in the center of it. *National Museum of the United States Air Force*

During the flight-testing phase of the XB-52's career, the aircraft is taking off from a desert airbase. There were four main landing gears, each with two wheels; two gears were positioned side-by-side forward, and two were aft. In addition, there was a retractable outrigger landing gear on each wing, to prevent the wingtips from striking the ground during takeoffs and landings. The main-gear wheels were steerable up to twenty degrees to the right or left, in order to manage the directional stability of the aircraft during landings and takeoffs in strong crosswinds. *National Archives*

With the exception of the very different noses and cockpit canopies, the XB-52 and the production B-52s were quite similar in shape. It was Gen. Curtis LeMay, commander of Strategic Air Command, who insisted on the discontinuation of the bubble canopies on production B-52s in favor of a redesigned canopy accommodating side-by-side pilot and copilot stations.
National Archives

Both of the outrigger landing gears are well above the tarmac in this right-rear view of the XB-52. The outrigger gears retracted inward into the wings; there was a landing-gear door on the outboard side of each of the lowered gears, and another door inboard of the outrigger gears, near the outboard engine nacelle. *National Museum of the United States Air Force*

Following several years of testing, mainly at Boeing Field, and later at Larson Air Force Base, Washington, the XB-52 was detailed to the Wright Air Development Center, at Wright-Patterson Air Force Base, Ohio, in 1957. The XB-52 is seen here at that base around 1958, during a period when the plane was being used as a testbed for a six-engine configuration: twin Pratt & Whitney J-57 turbojet engines on the inboard pylons and a single P&W J75 turbojet engine on each outboard pylon. At first glance, it seems that the dark-colored radomes had been replaced by white ones, but a close inspection of the photo shows that these actually may have been white covers for the radomes. The areas from the leading edges of the wings extending several feet onto the undersides of the wings have been painted white. *National Museum of the United States Air Force*

Northrop X-4 Bantam tail number 6677, a single-seat, swept-wing, semi-tailless aircraft that the National Advisory Committee for Aeronautics (NACA: the precursor of NASA) used for transonic testing, is parked next to the Boeing XB-52, with a B-36 in the background. Partially visible on the fuselage of the XB-52 just aft of the wings is a white cross on a black background, a pattern that was repeated on the opposite side of the fuselage. These were reference markings for a phototheodolite, an instrument for tracking the movements of the aircraft during takeoff and landing. The crosses visible on the tires evidently were for the same purpose. Similar markings were encountered on the YB-52.
National Museum of the United States Air Force

The white-cross reference marking for tracking by a phototheodolite is seen to better advantage in this view of the XB-52 flying low over the desert with its landing gear in the process of being lowered or retracted. The shape of the nonoperational tail turret is visible from this perspective. *National Museum of the United States Air Force*

The XB-52 flies past the summit of Mount Rainier, in Washington, during a test flight in the 1950s. Note the square window on the fuselage below the "STRATOFORTRESS" inscription: there was a similar one on the opposite side of the plane, and these were for the navigator and the radar operator. *National Museum of the United States Air Force*

The tandem cockpit arrangement of the XB-52, and the YB-52, with its fighter-type canopy, made for a sleek appearance, but it was foreseen that in operational service, the separation of the pilot and the copilot would be a serious, possibly fatal, flaw in the event of a failure of the intercom system.
National Museum of the United States Air Force

CHAPTER 2
YB-52

The YB-52, serial number 49-231, was a one-off service-test aircraft, virtually identical to the XB-52. This plane was rolled out of Boeing's Plant 2 in Seattle on March 15, 1952. Because the XB-52 was disabled by a rupture in the pneumatic system before its first flight, the YB-52 had its maiden flight before the XB-52, and one month after its rollout, on April 15, 1952. In this undated view, the YB-52 is taking off on a test flight. *National Archives*

The YB-52, serial number 49-231, rolled out of the Boeing plant on March 15, 1952, and took to the air one month later. That flight, from Boeing Field to Larson Air Force Base, Moses Lake, Washington was handled by Alvin M. "Tex" Johnson, Boeing's chief test pilot, and Lt. Col. Guy M. Townsend. The YB-52 lifted off at 11:08 am, flying for about forty minutes near the plant before climbing to 25,000 feet and making her way to the area of Larson Air Force Base, where a few more flight tests were run before the bomber landed at the base with a total flight time of three hours and eight minutes, the longest first flight in the company's history to that time.

Publically, Johnson and Townsend were enthusiastic about the big new bomber, but privately they expressed concerns about the high lateral control forces required. This situation was not entirely unexpected, as Boeing engineers had deliberately set the control forces as high as possible due to concerns about possible aileron overbalance. After resetting the forces required, the YB-52 was much easier to fly, and after only one week of flight testing in the sparsely populated Moses Lake area, the bomber returned to the Seattle area for further testing. On September 4, 1952, the same aircraft flew from Seattle to Dayton with an average speed of 624 miles per hour—which was faster than the average speed maintained by the F-86 on its 1952 Bendix Trophy-winning run!

Remarkably, the XB-52 and YB-52 came in slightly under the original design weight, which helped keep the planned performance estimates on track.

The inimitable Gen. Curtiss LeMay early on had voiced objections to the tandem cockpit arrangement found in the mockup and XB-52 and YB-52 aircraft. His concern had to do primarily with sharing the workload of the pilots. Beyond that, testing of the two initial aircraft showed some problems with downward visibility, although by that time plans were already in place for production aircraft to feature side by side seating for the pilot and copilot. With both the original and later style cockpits, the navigator and bombardier were situated beneath the pilot and copilot.

On January 27, 1958, after logging 783 flight hours, the historic YB-52 was donated to the Air Force Museum at Wright-Patterson Air Force Base, where it was placed on display. Unfortunately, during the late 1960s, the aircraft was scrapped.

The Boeing YB-52 is undergoing maintenance work in the foreground at Boeing Field, Seattle, Washington. Parked to the side of the YB-52 is Boeing B-47E-60-BW Stratojet, serial number 51-5219. Visible on the YB-52 is the tail number, 9231 (an abbreviated version of the serial number 49-231); the white cross on black background aft of the wing, for purposes of phototheodolite tracking; and the inscription "YB-52" in red below the cockpit. Note the reddish-brown coloration of both radomes on the nose, and the three red panels on the leading edge of the right wing. *National Archives*

This aerial photograph portrays in very graphic terms the changes that had been wrought in US strategic bombers in less than a decade, with the YB-52 dwarfing Boeing B-17G-55-BO Fortress, serial number 42-102588, converted to a B-17H search-and-rescue aircraft. The outboard and inboard Fowler-type flaps are extended on the YB-52. These flaps had a total area of 797 square feet. *National Museum of the United States Air Force*

The YB-52 flies high above a coastal area. Note the differing sheens of the metal on the various fuselage, wing, and empennage surfaces. The eleven round openings on the left side of the fuselage below and aft of the national insignia were a feature of the YB-52 and the X-52 but not of production B-52s. The openings were not repeated on the right side. *National Museum of the United States Air Force*

Evidence indicates that this photo of the YB-52 in flight was taken sometime before the middle of September 1954. Flight tests of the aircraft disclosed problems with the brakes. When approaching stall, the YB-52 tended to pitch upward and roll to the right. And, even normal throttle adjustments tended to make the Pratt & Whitney J57 engines race while at high altitude and with low engine-inlet temperature. These deficiencies would be fixed by the time the B-52 entered full production. *National Museum of the United States Air Force*

The YB-52 (right) undertakes a flight in company with a Boeing B-47 Stratojet (left). The YB-52 paved the way for the B-52s which, along with the B-47s, would constitute a large portion of the Strategic Air Command's nuclear strike force until the B-47s were retired as bomber aircraft in 1965. *National Museum of the United States Air Force*

Underwing auxiliary fuel tanks, as seen here, eventually were fitted to the YB-52. Following almost six years of flight testing, during which it logged 783 hours of flight, the YB-52 was sent to the United States Air Force Museum at Wright-Patterson Air Force Base, Ohio, in late January 1958, but the historically significant plane and the XB-52 were scrapped during the 1960s. *National Museum of the United States Air Force*

CHAPTER 3
B-52A

Originally, there were to have been thirteen examples of the first production version of the Stratofortress, the B-52, but ten of these airframes were diverted to serve as the first of the B-52Bs, leaving only three B-52As. Here, the first B-52A, serial number 52-001, has been rolled out of the assembly building at Boeing's Seattle plant in March 1954. The forty-eight-foot-tall vertical fin was folded down to the right to enable the bomber to clear the door of the assembly building. "B-52A" was painted in contemporary script on the sides of the forward fuselage. *National Museum of the United States Air Force*

On February 14, 1951, letter contract AF33(038)-21096 was signed, calling for the production of thirteen B-52A aircraft, the first of the type to include the side by side seating of the pilot and copilot requested by Gen. LeMay.

Other significant changes and improvements were the lengthening of the fuselage by four feet, the use of improved J57-P-9W engines, and the fitting of 1,000-gallon jettisonable fuel tanks on the outer wings. Inside, the crew increased to six, with a rear-facing electronic warfare officer seated behind the pilot, a gunner in his own compartment at the rear of the fuselage, and the navigator and radar operator beside each other on the fuselage lower deck. While the order for thirteen aircraft was consistent with the old standard of ordering thirteen service test aircraft, the order did not stand for long. On June 9, 1952, the contract was amended to just three B-52A aircraft, with the remaining ten to be B-52Bs.

The first B-52A, serial number 52-001, rolled out of Boeing's Seattle plant on March 18, 1954. It, along with the other two B-52As, serial numbers 52-002 and 52-003, were the first Stratofortresses to be equipped with armament, a four .50-caliber machine gun installation in the tail. The gunner was to use an A-3A fire control system to aim and fire the guns, each of which was fed with 600 rounds of ammunition.

Although considered production aircraft, the B-52A models in fact were not fit for service in operational units, as they lacked many of the electronic systems, not the least of which were the bombing and navigation systems. The aircraft were ultimately used as test and development aircraft, with the final B-52A, 52-003, being modified in November 1958, to become a mother ship for the X-15 rocket plane. At that time the bomber was reclassified as NB-52A. This conversion included adding a pylon beneath the inner starboard wing for supporting the X-15 prior to launch. The NB-52A was retired in October 1969, and is now on display at the Pima Air Museum in Tucson; it is the oldest surviving B-52.

The first B-52A, serial number 52-001 (and tail number 2001), makes a flight above the Northwest coast. Like the XB-52 and the YB-52, this aircraft had the white crosses on a black background aft of the wings: reference markings for use with a phototheodolite to establish the points where the plane's wheels left the runway during takeoffs, or touched down during landings. The US Air Force accepted this first B-52A in June 1954, and immediately bailed it back to Boeing for the purposes of testing the aircraft. Although from many angles the B-52 may be considered a graceful, even sleek aircraft, it was perhaps its sheer size, slab-sided fuselage, and low stance when on the ground that earned it the nickname "BUFF," which stood for Big, Ugly, Fat F****r, sometimes rendered as Big, Ugly, Fat Fellow. "BUFF" rather than "Stratofortress" was the moniker of preference for the big bomber's flight crews and ground personnel. *National Museum of the United States Air Force*

The third and last B-52A, serial number 52-003, lacks the "Boeing B-52A Stratofortress" inscription on the forward fuselage in this photo taken during a test flight from Edwards Air Force Base, California, sometime before November 3, 1955. In addition to having a redesigned cockpit and canopy, the B-52As had the forward fuselage extended by four feet. Boeing used the third B-52A for general flight-test purposes until late 1958, when the aircraft was converted to the NB-52A, in which role it was used as a mothership for the North American X-15, the joint USAF/NASA experimental rocket-powered, high-speed research aircraft. *National Archives*

Boeing B-52A, serial number 52-003, is viewed from the lower left during a flight. The B-52As had operable tail turrets with four .50-caliber machine guns, operated by a tail gunner who was located in the tail. The three B-52As were powered by eight Pratt & Whitney J57-P-1W turbojet engines with water injection: a feature that enabled the engines to have brief bursts of extra power, such as during takeoffs. Each engine was rated at 10,000 pounds static thrust (lbst) without water injection and 11,000 lbst with water injection. *National Archives*

The same plane, B-52A, serial number 52-003, is viewed from the upper right from a chase plane during a test flight out of Edwards Air Force Base prior to late March 1955. The first flight of a B-52A (52-001) was on August 5, 1954. Technically, the three B-52As were designated B-52A-1-BO, the suffix 1 referring to Block 1, and "BO" standing for Boeing, Seattle. *National Archives*

The white-cross reference marking on the right side of the fuselage is prominent in this in-flight photo of the third B-52A during a flight near Edwards Air Force Base sometime before late March 1955. Note the anti-glare matte black finish on the upper part of the tail turret aft of the tail gunner's canopy.
National Archives

A North American F-100 Super Sabre chase plane accompanies a Boeing B-52A on a flight over the Mojave Desert in California during the mid-1950s. Note the dark paint on the B-52A's wingtips. Auxiliary fuel tanks are mounted under the outer parts of the wings; each one had a 700-gallon capacity.
National Archives

The third B-52A has just landed at Edwards Air Force Base, California, on October 19, 1955. The drag chute has been deployed to help the plane come to a stop before running out of runway. The lift exerted on the wings is keeping the outrigger landing gear well above the surface of the runway. On the fuselage, aft of the number 003, is the insignia of the Air Force Flight Test Center at Edwards Air Force Base. *National Archives*

At first glance, this official photograph seems to show all three B-52As flying together in formation, as the tail number of the third B-52A, 2003, is clearly visible on the nearest aircraft. However, upon viewing the tail number of the second plane, 2000, which was a nonexistent number for a B-52, suspicions arose. A very close examination of the second and third planes reveals that they are identical in perspective and details to the first plane. This image clearly is a composite photo.
National Museum of the United States Air Force

The third B-52A, serial number 52-003, was converted to the NB-52A and served as one of two motherships for the X-15s and experimental lifting bodies. (The other mothership was NB-52B, serial number 52-008, nicknamed "The Challenger" and later "Balls 8.") In that role, the NB-52A had the nickname "The High and Mighty One," as well as "Balls 3," based on its -003 serial-number suffix. Here, an X-15 with external fuel tanks is mounted on the pylon under the right wing of the NB-52A. A notch was cut in the trailing edge of the wing to provide clearance for the X-15's vertical tail.
National Museum of the United States Air Force

During one of its early missions for NASA, the NB-52A is carrying an X-15 aloft. Below the cockpit canopy is the insignia of the Air Research and Development Command. Above the US Air Force inscription on the fuselage is a blister with a window on its rear, above which is a square window, which was replaced by a bubble window in the period between the X-15's first glide flight and its first powered flight. The inscription "The High and Mighty One" would be applied to the fuselage later. *NASA*

The first X-15, serial number 56-6670, has just been released from the NB-52A for its first unpowered flight, on June 8, 1959. The tail turret of the NB-52A had been removed, and the resulting opening in the tail had a flat fairing over it. The housing for the tail gunner's periscopic sight and the tail radome remained, causing a noticeable protrusion on the upper part of the tail of the fuselage: one of the features that distinguished the NB-52A from the NB-52B. There were areas of orange Day-Glo paint on the forward fuselage, the vertical tail, and the fronts of the engine nacelles. *National Museum of the United States Air Force*

"The High and Mighty One," Boeing NB-52A, serial number 52-0008, is rolling out to its takeoff position with an X-15 mounted on the wing pylon, at Edwards Air Force Base, California, on May 22, 1962. The bubble window now was present on the NB-52A's fuselage, above the teardrop-shaped fairing to the front of the wing. By this stage, the side of the fuselage to the lower front of the right wing was getting full of a scorecard for X-15 missions. *National Archives*

The Boeing NB-52A takes off from Edwards Air Force Base on July 17, 1962, carrying an X-15 with Maj. Robert M. White, USAF, as pilot. On this day, White became the first man to fly a winged aircraft into space, thus achieving the status of astronaut. He reached an altitude of 314,750 feet—59.6 miles—over Edwards Air Force Base. *National Archives*

Flying over Edwards Air Force Base, California, on November 3, 1965, the NB-52A nicknamed "The High and Mighty One" is carrying under its right wing the second X-15, later X-15A-2, serial number 56-6671, equipped with the under-fuselage auxiliary fuel tanks that recently had been introduced. The NB-52A survives and is on display at the Pima Air & Space Museum, Tucson, Arizona. *National Archives*

An Air Force officer and a civilian in a hardhat look on as the NB-52A takes to the air on an X-15 mission on August 29, 1962. A very close examination of the aircraft reveals that the periscopic gun sight and the tail radome, remnants of the now-removed tail turret, are present: proof that this was the NB-52A, not the NB-52B. To the right is the NASA control van, with radio equipment for maintaining communications with all units involved in the X-15 test flights. *National Archives*

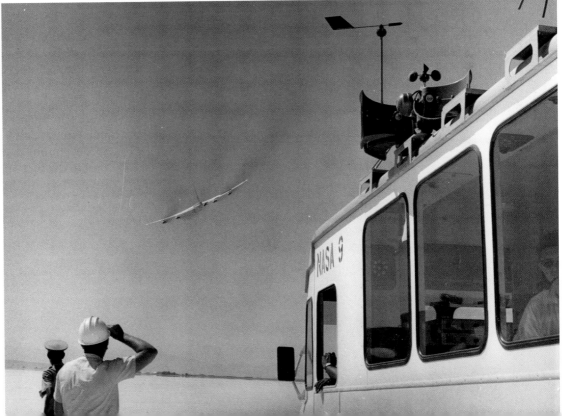

CHAPTER 4
B-52B

Fifty examples of the B version of the B-52 were built, with twenty-three being B-52Bs and twenty-seven as RB-52Bs, dual-purpose bomber/reconnaissance aircraft. The B models were the first combat-ready, fully operational model of the Stratofortress and were similar to the B-52A, with the addition of an operational bombing/navigation system. Shown here is the second B-model plane, RB-52B-5-BO, serial number 52-0005, at Edwards Air Force Base in 1955. The insignia of the Air Force Flight Test Center is below the cockpit canopy. *National Archives*

As mentioned in the previous chapter, the initial contract for thirteen B-52A aircraft was modified in June 1952, to specify three B-52A aircraft and ten B-52B aircraft. At that time, a further seven B-52Bs were added to that contract. An additional contract was signed on April 15, 1953, for a further forty-two B-52Bs equipped for reconnaissance work, designated RB-52B. A year later that contract was modified, reducing the number of RB-52Bs on the order to thirty-three, with the other ten aircraft to be B-52Cs instead. Ultimately, ten of the aircraft on this contract were built as RB-52B, as well as all seventeen aircraft remaining on the previous contract.

The RB-52B differed from the B-52B in that the bomb bay was equipped to handle a pressurized crew capsule housing two reconnaissance operators and the equipment they were to use. This equipment could be either electronic countermeasures or photographic reconnaissance gear. The equipment could vary, depending upon mission needs, and could include an AN/APR-14 low-frequency radar receiver; two AN/APR-9 high-frequency radar receivers; two AN/APA-11A pulse analyzers; and three AN/ARR-88 panoramic receivers. An AN/ANQ-1A wire recorder was provided to record the data produced by the equipment. Photo reconnaissance equipment could include four K-38 cameras in the multi-camera station as well as either a T-11 or K-36 camera at the vertical camera station. Three T-11s could also be mounted for cartographic work. Photoflash bombs could be carried and dropped to aid in photography. The two-man capsule crew were provided with downward-firing ejection seats.

During the course of production, a number of engine types were factory installed on the B-52B/RB-52B series aircraft, including the J57-P-1W, -1WA, -1WB, J57-P-29W, J57-P-29WA, and the J57-P-19W.

Another area of aircraft-to-aircraft variation was the tail gun installation. Nine of the initial RB-52Bs were equipped, as planned, with the A-3A .50-caliber quadruple machine gun mounting. However, one of the B-52B aircraft, 52-009, was equipped with an MD-5 fire control system and a pair of M24A-1 20 mm autocannons. The MD-5 was also installed on the remainder of the RB-52Bs as well as sixteen B-52Bs, serial numbers 53-0366 thru 53-0391. The final group of seven B-52Bs used the intended A-3A system.

Although it was intended that the MA-2 bombing and navigation system be installed in the aircraft, developmental delays led to the K-3A system, designed by Sperry for the B-36, being installed instead. The higher operational altitudes of the B-52 led to problems with this installation, with the result being inaccurate bombing.

The first B-52B flight was on January 25, 1955, and the final B-52B was delivered in August 1956. B-52B 57-8711 was delivered to the 93rd Bomb Wing at Castle Air Force Base, Merced, California, on June 29, 1955, beginning that nuclear-armed wing's conversion from a B-47 unit to the first operational B-52 unit.

B/RB-52B Serial Numbers	
52-004/006	Boeing RB-52B-5-BO Stratofortress
52-007/013	Boeing RB-52B-10-BO Stratofortress
52-8710/8715	Boeing RB-52B-15-BO Stratofortress
52-8716	Boeing RB-52B-20-BO Stratofortress
53-366/372	Boeing RB-52B-25-BO Stratofortress
53-373/376	Boeing B-52B-25-BO Stratofortress
53-377/379	Boeing RB-52B-30-BO Stratofortress
53-380/387	Boeing B-52B-30-BO Stratofortress
53-388/398	Boeing B-52B-35-BO Stratofortress

Boeing RB-52B-5-BO, serial number 52-0005, is viewed from the left front at Edwards Air Force Base in 1955. The B-model Stratofortresses had an upgraded engine: the Pratt & Whitney J57-P-19W with water injection, rated at 10,000 lbst. For the RB-52Bs, a pressurized reconnaissance capsule was developed, which could be mounted in a bomb bay. This capsule came in several configurations that included mapping and reconnaissance camera arrays, mapping radar, weather-recon equipment, electronic intelligence (ELINT), and electronic countermeasures (ECM) gear, and stations for two crewmen: one to operate the high-frequency recon equipment and one for the low-frequency electronic recon suite. *National Archives*

Whereas most RB-52Bs had a tail turret containing two 20 mm cannons, RB-52B-BO-5, serial number 52-0005, had the same quad-.50-caliber gun turret as the B-52A and the B-52B. It was one of nine early RB-52Bs armed with quad-.50s. The photo was taken at Edwards Air Force Base in 1955. *National Archives*

Boeing RB-52B-5-BO, serial number 52-0005, is viewed from the left rear at Edwards Air Force Base. The right outrigger wheel is touching the tarmac, while the left outrigger wheel is slightly above the tarmac. *National Archives*

The third B-model Stratofortress, RB-52B-5-BO, serial number 52-0006, is parked on a hardstand at an unidentified airbase on February 23, 1956. For the RB-52B and the B-52B, 1,000-gallon drop tanks were developed. Note how the forward main landing gear doors are steered to the right. *National Archives*

Boeing RB-52B-10-BO serial number 52-0012 is parked at Eglin Air Force Base, Florida, in or around May 1956. This was one of the nine early RB-52Bs to be armed with four .50-caliber machine guns in the tail turret. *National Archives*

Also seen at Eglin Air Force Base, but in or before July 1955, is RB-52B-10-BO, serial number 52-0011. A fairly good view of the 1,000-gallon under-wing auxiliary fuel tank is available; note how the rear of the tank slopes upward in a steady curve. This BUFF was retired to the Military Aircraft Storage and Disposition Center (MASDC) at Davis-Monthan Air Force Base, Tucson, Arizona, on June 8, 1966, and was declared excess on January 15, 1969. *National Archives*

Maintenance work is being performed on RB-52B-10-BO, serial number 52-0012, at Eglin Air Force Base; the photo was taken before July 5, 1955, by the 3206th Test Wing (Technical Support). The lower radome has been removed from the nose, and some of the access doors on the engine nacelles are open.
National Archives

On a mid-1950s flight out of Eglin Air Force Base, RB-52B-10-BO, serial number 52-0012, has its left outrigger landing gear lowered. At the time, this Stratofortress was undergoing tests to establish its maximum internal weapons load. The bomb bay doors had been removed, and the bomb bays were fitted with the reconnaissance capsule. *National Archives*

The same plane, RB-52B-10-BO, serial number 52-0012, is viewed from slightly above the right side, again during a flight out of Eglin Air Force Base in the mid-1950s during experiments to determine maximum internal weapons load. *National Archives*

A B-47E Stratojet is accompanying RB-52B-19-BO, serial number 52-0012, during a flight from Eglin Air Force Base during maximum-ordnance-load tests in the mid-1950s. The left outrigger landing gear is still lowered: the wheel is visible beneath the belly of the RB-52B. *National Archives*

Boeing RB-52B-15-BO, serial number 52-8715, conducts a training mission near Castle Air Force Base, California, on February 1, 1956. This aircraft was assigned to the 93rd Bombardment Group, based at Castle Air Force Base, Merced, California. This was the first group to be equipped with RB-52Bs, and it served largely as a training unit for Stratofortress crews. The sash and shield of Strategic Air Command (SAC) are in an unusual position on the rear fuselage; usually these markings were on the forward fuselage. *National Archives*

Boeing RB-52B-5-BO, serial number 52-0005, comes in for a landing. The SAC shield and sash are on their typical location on the forward fuselage. This RB-52B served as a test aircraft for its first six months and then was assigned to the 93rd Bombardment Wing at Castle Air Force Base, California, where it continued to serve until it was turned over to the 3415th Maintenance and Supply Group, Lowry Air Force Base, Colorado, in 1966. There, this plane was used as a training aircraft. *National Museum of the United States Air Force*

Boeing RB-52B-10-BO, serial number 52-0009, rolls to a drag-chute-assisted stop upon landing at an unidentified airfield. The last digit of the serial number and the tail number, "9," is stenciled on the nose. *National Museum of the United States Air Force*

Seven Stratofortresses are visible in this view of a flightline at an unidentified airbase. The nearest aircraft is RB-52B-20-BO, serial number 52-8716, and the next one in line is RB-52B-15-BO, serial number 52-8715. Both of these aircraft have the twin 20 mm gun mounts in the tail turrets. All of the Stratofortresses with fuselage bellies visible have had Gloss White reflective paint applied to the bellies, to reflect heat and radiation from nuclear blasts. The wing and horizontal stabilizer/elevator bottoms, engine nacelles and pylons, and external fuel tanks were similarly painted.
National Archives

Parked on a tarmac in Wichita, Kansas, sometime before July 7, 1956, are, left, Boeing B-52B-30-BO, serial number 53-0377, and, right, Boeing B-52B-35-BO, serial number 53-0391. Both planes are finished in natural metal, with Gloss White on the lower surfaces. Starting with the B-52D, the Wichita plant would share Stratofortress production with Boeing's Seattle plant.
National Archives

Eleven Stratofortresses from the 93rd Bombardment Group (Heavy) are in view in this photograph taken at Castle Air Force Base around early 1956. In the foreground is serial number 53-0388, the first of eleven B-52B-35-BOs, which were the final production block of the B-52Bs. A tractor is preparing to tow this bomber to a hangar. *National Archives*

In a view of three B-model Stratofortresses on a flightline at Castle Air Force Base, the closest one has its vertical fin and rudder folded to the side, and jack stands are installed at several points under the wings. Zinc chromate primer is visible on the bottom edge of the fin/rudder assembly. *National Archives*

A row of Stratofortresses are parked on a tarmac at Castle Air Force Base, California, on February 1, 1956. The first four planes were all part of the B-52B-30-BO production block. From closest to farthest, they are serial numbers 53-0380, 53-0382, 53-0381, and 53-0384. Note the apparent abrasion to the white paint on the underside of the right wing of the first plane, and the erosion of the white paint on the radomes of the first two aircraft. *National Archives*

In addition to the third B-52A, serial number 52-003, nicknamed "Balls 3" and "The High and Mighty One," the Air Force and NASA used one other Stratofortress as a mothership in the X-15 program: Boeing RB-52B-10-BO, serial number 52-0008, which was nicknamed "Balls 8" after the last digit of its serial number. Wearing NASA markings on its vertical tail, "Balls 8" is seen here during an open house at an airfield. *National Museum of the United States Air Force*

At Edwards Air Force Base on August 6, 1963, the first X-15, serial number 56-6670, is mounted on the pylon under the right wing of "Balls 8." A small part of the X-15's rear fuselage and vertical tail, including the tail number, is visible below the wing. *National Archives*

Main landing-gear doors nearly closed, the NB-52B lifts off from Edwards Air Force Base on a mission to launch an X-15. Day-Glo Orange paint is on the top of the nose and on a band around the rear fuselage, for high visibility. *National Museum of the United States Air Force*

A NASA-marked crash truck, utility pickup truck, and panel-delivery truck are standing by the flightline at Edwards Air Force Base, with the NB-52B parked in the left background. An X-15 is mounted on a pylon underneath the right wing. In the background is the NB-52A also with an X-15 mounted under the wing. *NASA*

The Boeing NB-52B, serial number 52-0008, is prepared for takeoff at Edwards Air Force Base on May 3, 1968. On the right-wing pylon is the payload for the day: the Northrop HL-10 experimental lifting-body aircraft. This day's mission marked the fifth flight for the HL-10, and it would be an unpowered glide, with test pilot Jerauld Gentry at the controls. Note the straight profile of the rear of the fuselage where the tail turret has been removed, with an observation canopy at the top. On the NB-52A, the gun sight housing from the old tail turret remained in place above the faired-over location where the tail turret had been removed. This created a prominent protrusion at the top of the tail of the fuselage which helps to differentiate the NB-52A from the NB-52B. *National Archives*

The Boeing NB-52B is acting as the mothership for the Northrop M2-F3 heavyweight lifting body (NASA number 803) during a flight out of Edwards Air Force Base on May 22, 1970. The M2-F3 was rebuilt from the Northrop M2-F2 after that aircraft crashed in 1967. Above the "US AIR FORCE" inscription on the fuselage is the scorecard for experimental-aircraft missions, with horizontal silhouettes indicating powered flights and downward-pointing silhouettes standing for unpowered or glide flights. *National Archives*

The one-off Martin Marietta X-24B experimental lifting body has just been launched from the Boeing NB-52B on October 4, 1973. Below the cockpit canopy is the insignia of the US Air Force Flight Test Center at Edwards Air Force Base. Research on the lifting bodies in the 1960s and 1970s would prove very important in the design and development of the Space Shuttle. *National Archives*

NASA's NB-52B is configured here as the mothership for NASA's X-43 experimental, unmanned, hypervelocity aircraft, part of the Hyper-X program. Under the right wing is the adapter on which the X-43 was mounted. Flight tests of the X-43A using the NB-52B as the mothership occurred in the early 2000s. *NASA*

A NASA F/A-18 chase plane accompanies the NB-52B "Balls 8." During its long career as a NASA mothership, spanning from the fifth launching of the X-15 in January 1960, until its retirement in December 2004. "Balls 8" continues as a display aircraft at Edwards Air Force Base. *NASA*

The Boeing NB-52B, "Balls 8," is on the runway at Edwards Air Force Base. The format of the tail number varied over time: here, it is 008. The prominent cutout in the trailing edge of the right wing, for accommodating the vertical tail of the X-15 and subsequent experimental aircraft, is visible. *NASA*

The NB-52B is in motion on the runway at Edwards Air Force Base, its wings swooping upward in a noticeable curve and the outrigger landing gear wheels well above the runway. *NASA*

This close-up of the right side of the fuselage of the Boeing NB-52B shows the extensive scoreboard, documenting the missions in which this aircraft was the mothership for various experimental aircraft. *NASA*

Boeing RB-52B-10-BO, serial number 50-013, is shown over the Pacific Proving Ground during the May 21, 1956, "Cherokee" thermonuclear test at Bikini Atoll. On that date, this Stratofortress performed the first drop of a live hydrogen bomb. Due to a navigational error, the crew dropped the device four miles from its target, which invalidated the test data and endangered a number of spectators.
National Archives

Tragedy struck a Stratofortress and its crew on April 7, 1961, when a live AIM-9B Sidewinder air-to-air missile on the F-100 Super Sabre fighter jet shown here was accidentally fired at the aircraft during a training mission over Mount Taylor, New Mexico. The Sidewinder detonated on an engine on the left wing of RB-52B-30-BO, serial number 53-0380, nicknamed *Ciudad Juarez* and assigned to the 95th Bombardment Wing at Biggs Air Force Base, El Paso, Texas. The firing of the missile apparently was not the result of pilot error. *National Archives*

Crewmen of a Kaman HH-43 Huskie helicopter are removing SSgt. Manuel Mieras, crewchief of *Ciudad Juarez,* for emergency surgery at a hospital at Sandia, New Mexico. Sgy.Mieras lost a leg in the disaster. All of the other survivors suffered various injuries. *National Archives*

Among the wreckage of *Ciudad Juarez*, on a mountainside in western New Mexico, is a section of fuselage with the plane's nickname painted on it. The remains of three members of the crew were found in the wreckage. The pilot, Capt. Donald Blodgett, and four other members of the crew were able to eject from the bomber, and they all survived. *National Archives*

Students are loading multiple ejector racks on the pylons of RB-52B-5-BO, serial number 52-0005, being used as a trainer aircraft, at Lowry Air Force Base, Denver, Colorado, in October 1970. While used as a training airframe, possibly as early as when this photo was taken, this aircraft was redesignated a GB-52B. The airframe was retired in 1982, and it is currently on display at Wings over the Rockies Air Museum, located at the former Lowry Air Force Base. *National Archives*

CHAPTER 5
B-52C

The B-52Cs were produced at Boeing's Seattle plant; a total of thirty-five examples were completed. The principal change in the external appearance of the C model from the B was the introduction of the 3,000-gallon underwing fuel tanks, which were noticeably larger than the 1,000-gallon tanks of the previous models of the B-52. The first flight for a B-52C was on March 9, 1956. The first C-model Stratofortress, B-52C-40-BO, serial number 53-0399, is shown here prior to taking off on a test flight at Edwards Air Force Base on October 20, 1957. *National Archives*

Production of the B-52C was called for in the September 1952 Letter Contract F33(600)-22119. This contract was originally for RB-52Bs, but was amended in May of 1954, to make the final ten aircraft on the contract B-52Cs instead. Although designated simply B-52C, these aircraft had the same provisions to carry the reconnaissance pod as did the B-52B.

The C model differed externally from its predecessors most notably in having provisions for 3,000-gallon underwing fuel tanks in lieu of the 1,000-gallon tanks of the earlier models. This change brought the fuel capacity to 41,700 gallons—which along with other changes raised the gross weight to 450,000 pounds. The powerplants were the same as those used on the late production B-52B aircraft. The other notable change to the outside of the aircraft was the application of white paint to the underside. The intent of this was that in the event the aircraft was in fact used to deliver nuclear ordnance, as it was intended to do, the white paint would aid in reflecting the bomb blast heat away from the aircraft as it turned toward home.

As the result of the crash of a B-52B, which was traced to an air turbine-powered alternator, the B-52C was equipped with new design alternators with improved bearings.

Only thirty-five B-52Cs were built before production shifted to the B-52D. All of these were produced in Boeing's Seattle plant, and the B-52C was the final B-52 model produced exclusively at that facility. The B-52C was retired in 1971.

B-52C Serial Numbers

53-0399/0408	Boeing B-52C-40-BO Stratofortress
54-2664/2675	Boeing B-52C-45-BO Stratofortress
54-2676/2688	Boeing B-52C-50-BO Stratofortress

The first of the C-model planes, B-52C-40-BO, serial number 53-0399, makes a flight near Edwards Air Force Base, California, on October 18, 1957. It is curious that the first production block for the B-52Cs was 40 and not the usual number 1, but this seems to have been a continuation from the last production block of the B-52B/RB-52B, number 35. (Production blocks typically started at 1, followed by 5 and increments of 5.) This plane has a large, white cross on a black background on each side of the fuselage aft of the wings, as a highly visible aiming point for cameras during flight testing. *National Archives*

Boeing B-52C-40-BO, serial number 53-0400, the second of the C-model Stratofortresses, cruises high above the clouds sometime before late July 1956. Although some B-52Bs and RB-52Bs had received Gloss White paint on the undersides to reflect radiation and heat from nuclear blasts, after they went into service, the B-52Cs were the first Stratofortresses to receive this paint treatment at the factory. *National Archives*

Maintenance personnel are preparing Boeing B-52C-40-BO, serial number 53-0405, in a hangar at Loring Air Force Base, Maine, for the annual Strategic Air Command bombing-navigation competition on September 7 , 1956. A red stripe is painted below the tail number. On the bottom of the fuselage just forward of the tail turret is the box for the forty-eight-foot ribbon-canopy drag chute; the box is in its lowered position. To the immediate front of the drag-chute box is an open access door. *National Archives*

This is claimed to have been the first officially released photograph of a B-52C. It shows the second plane in that model, B-52C-40-BO, serial number 53-0400. It served until being placed in storage at Davis-Monthan Air Force Base, Arizona, in late September 1971. All four flaps are lowered, imparting a good sense of their massive sizes. *National Museum of the United States Air Force*

The last of the ten B-52Cs of the 040 production block, serial number 53-0408, takes off from Loring Air Force Base, Maine, during the annual Strategic Air Command bombing-navigation competition, on September 13, 1956. It had been only six months since the first flight of a B-52C. The SAC bombing competitions had begun in 1948, and these annual events grew to include navigation, aerial refueling, and munitions-loading competitions, to name a few. *National Archives*

Boeing B-52C-45-BO, serial number 54-2665, is being prepared for a mission during the SAC competition at Loring Air Force Base on September 13, 1956. This Stratofortress, which recently had entered service, is in very clean condition. The B-52Cs first entered operational service with the 42nd Bombardment Wing at Loring Air Force Base in June 1956. *National Archives*

A tanker is refueling Boeing B-52C-45-BO, serial number 54-2664, at Loring Air Force Base. The Strategic Air Command shield and sash are on the nose, and the last four digits of the serial number are stenciled to the rear of the lower radome. Two other B-52Cs, including B-52C-50-BO, serial number 54-2684, to the left, are in the background. *National Museum of the United States Air Force*

A tractor is towing B-52C-45-BO, serial number 54-2673, to a position at an unidentified site, most likely Loring Air Force Base. In the left background, mostly hidden by the tractor, is a second B-52C, serial number 53-0400. The tail number of that plane, 3400, is also stenciled on the 3,000-gallon underwing fuel tank. *National Museum of the United States Air Force*

Ground crewmen are working on a B-52C at Loring Air Force Base on September 27, 1956, during the Strategic Air Command competitions. While the SAC shield was on the left side of the nose, the insignia of the 42nd Bombardment Wing was on the right side of the nose, along with the blue sash with white stars. *National Archives*

The impressive proportions of the wingspan of the Stratofortress are readily visible in this photograph of a B-52C undergoing maintenance work at Loring Air Force on September 27, 1956. The Gloss White anti-radiation paint treatment on the undersides of the aircraft included the lower radome, while the upper radome retained its dark coloration. Red covers are installed over the inlets of all but the two right outboard engines. *National Archives*

CHAPTER 6
B-52D

Whereas only thirty-five B-52Cs were produced, the B-52D was the first model of the Stratofortress to be issued in a large production lot, with a total of 170 examples being manufactured from June 1956 to November 1957. The D model was virtually identical in external appearance to the C model. The main difference between the models was that the B-52Ds were equipped with the MD-9 fire-control system, which had been installed in the final B-52C, and the B-52Ds were the first model to be modified for low-level bombing operations. The B-52Ds also were the first model of BUFF built at Boeing's Wichita, Kansas, plant in addition to the Seattle plant, and the D-model Stratofortresses would see extensive service as conventional bombers in the Vietnam War. Seen here is B-52D-70-BO, serial number 56-0586, prepared to fly a SAC mission during Operation Head Start at Loring Air Force Base, Maine, on December 10, 1958. *National Archives*

The B-52D was in essence a B-52C without the capability of carrying the reconnaissance capsule. Production of the B-52D was carried out at both the Seattle plant where the earlier Stratofortresses had been assembled, as well as the Boeing Wichita plant, which was winding down B-47 production. Production of the two models overlapped, in that Wichita completed the first B-52D, serial number 55-0049, on December 7, 1955, the same day that Boeing Seattle completed the first B-52C. In time, B-52 production in Seattle would be phased out entirely, freeing up space at that plant for the increasing civilian-pattern aircraft production.

The first flight of a B-52D was on May 14, 1956. The first flight of a Seattle-built B-52D did not occur until September 28, 1956. The aircraft from the two plants were differentiated in documents through the plant code abbreviation in the aircraft production block identifier, with –BO indicating Seattle and –BW indicating Wichita. As built, the B-52D differed little from the B-52C, with the chief difference being the previously mentioned lack of provisions to accommodate a reconnaissance capsule.

However, soon after the B-52Ds began to enter service, which began with the 42nd Bomb Wing at Loring Air Force Base, Maine, the B-52Ds began to be modified. Some of these modifications were to remedy identified problems with the water injection system—utilized to cool the engine intake air and thus increase takeoff power, icing in the fuel system, and fuel system leaks.

As the war in Vietnam escalated, the B-52 began to be used in that conflict as a conventional bomber, a role for which it was never intended. While the initial type used in Southeast Asia was the B-52F, soon additional aircraft were required, and the plentiful B-52D, of which 170 had been produced, was a natural choice.

As built, however, the B-52D could handle only twenty-seven conventional bombs—which were well below the weight limit for the bomber. In December 1965, Project Big Belly began, which modified the internal arrangement of equipment so that forty-two 750-pound M117 conventional bombs or eighty-four Mk.82 500-pound bombs could be carried in the bomb bay. A further twenty-four bombs of either type could be carried externally on racks originally developed for the Hound Dog missile. These changes brought the payload to 60,000 pounds, a significant increase over that of the B-52F.

The aircraft also gained a new color scheme, with tan and two-tone green camouflage replacing the glistening natural finish of the upper surfaces, and glossy black, better for hiding from searchlights, replacing the glossy white previously applied to the bottoms.

At Loring Air Force Base during Operation Head Start on a chilly December 10, 1958, the tail assembly and the tail turret of a Stratofortress are viewed from a close vantage point. The tail number, 50049, correlates to serial number 55-0049, the first B-52D-1-BW, the "BW" suffix standing for Boeing, Wichita. The drag-chute box is in its open position below the rear of the fuselage. Also the tail turret is depressed to about its lower limit. *National Archives*

A USAF GAM-72 Quail air-launched decoy missile ("GAM" was the acronym for "Guided Aircraft Missile") is resting on a hoisting truck next to B-52D-40-BW, serial number 56-0695. The B-52D was equipped to carry either the GAM-72 Quail subsonic decoy missile or the GAM-77 Hound Dog supersonic cruise missile. Up to eight of these missiles could be carried in the B-52D's bomb bay, but the normal complement was two. The Hound Dogs, on the other hand, were carried on under-wing pylons. The Quail was designed to mimic the radar profile of the B-52 and thus confuse, and hopefully defeat, enemy air defenses.
National Archives

B-52Ds are parked at Loring Air Force Base in the late afternoon of a winter day in 1958. Snow covers much of the wings and middle fuselage of the plane in the left foreground, Wichita-built B-52D-15-BW, serial number 55-0064. In the right foreground is the tail of B-52D-15-BW serial number 55-0061. Note the covers secured over the tail turrets to protect them from the elements.
National Archives

A Stratofortress is parked on a snowy hardstand at Loring Air Force Base, Maine, on December 10, 1958, prior to a mission related to Operation Head Start, a Strategic Air Command exercise held from September to December 1958. This exercise was tested to assess the ability of B-52s flying from Loring Air Force Base to maintain a continuous airborne nuclear alert above the Atlantic off the western coast of Greenland. These flights typically lasted twenty hours and required precise planning, maintenance, logistics, and coordination. Live nuclear weapons were carried. *National Archives*

Boeing B-52D-70-BO, serial number 56-0586, is taxiing at Loring Air Force Base, Maine, during Operation Head Start on December 10, 1958. An adaptation of the serial number, 6586, is stenciled on the auxiliary fuel tank and on the fuselage just aft of the lower radome. On the nose is the SAC sash, a blue band with white stars. *National Archives*

On June 26, 1958, a crew chief at Loring Air Force Base made the mistake of attempting to start the engines of a parked B-52D-60-BO, serial number 55-0102, of the 42nd Bombardment Wing, without first pulling the proper circuit breaker. This caused a spark, which ignited a fuel leak, and the plane went up in flames. *National Archives*

B-52D-60-BO, serial number 55-0102, is viewed from a different angle as it burns on the tarmac at Loring Air Force Base on June 26, 1958. No personnel were lost or injured in this accident. The plane was written off as damaged beyond repair. *National Archives*

Maintenance crewmen are working on Boeing B-52D-40-BW, serial number 56-0692, at Ellsworth Air Force Base, South Dakota, during an operational readiness inspection at some point in or before mid-May 1973. Faintly visible on the SAC sash on the nose is the insignia of the 28th Bombardment Wing. This B-52D survives, and is on display at Tinker Air Force Base, Oklahoma City, Oklahoma. *National Archives*

Seattle-built B-52D-80-BO, serial number 56-0620, was assigned throughout its whole career to the Air Force Special Weapons Center (AFSWC) at Kirtland Air Force Base, New Mexico, where it was engaged in the test-dropping of inert nuclear bombs. By the late 1980s, this Stratofortress had been placed into long-term storage at Davis-Monthan Air Force Base, Arizona. *National Museum of the United States Air Force*

The tail turret of a B-52D is viewed close-up from the left side. The housing containing the four .50-caliber machine guns was articulated, with the aft section swiveling up and down, and the forward section traversing from side to side. Between the four machine-gun barrels was the black radome of the tracking antenna. Above the gun mount was the white radome for a search antenna, above which was the clear hemispheric cover for the objective of the gunner's periscopic sight. The white protrusion below the gunner's canopy was the antenna for the APS-54 tail-warning radar; there was a similar antenna on the opposite side of the tail. *National Museum of the United States Air Force*

When B-52Ds were sent to Southeast Asia for use as conventional bombers in the Vietnam War, they were painted in a camouflage scheme of Dark Green (FS 34079), SAC Bomber Green (FS 34159), and SAC Tan (FS 24201 or 34201) on the upper surfaces, and Black (FS 17038 or 27030) on the sides and bottom surfaces. This undated photo taken at an unidentified airbase shows such a B-52D. The Big Belly program provided B-52Ds with under-wing multiple ejector racks, as seen here. Big Belly allowed the B-52Ds to carry a greatly increased load of conventional bombs in the bomb bay (for example, up to eighty-four 500-pound Mk.82 bombs) and up to twenty-four bombs, either 500-pound or 750-pound, on multiple ejector racks. *National Archives*

A B-52 loaded with Mk.82 500-pound bombs on the multiple ejector racks has just taken to the air on a bombing mission over Vietnam. Developed during the 1950s, the Mk.82 500-pound bombs saw extensive use in the conflict in Southeast Asia in the 1960s and 1970s. When fitted with a folding-fin retarder, the Mk.82 became the Snakeye high-drag bomb, useful in low-altitude bombing missions to prevent blast damage to the aircraft. *National Archives*

Boeing's Wichita Division devised this package concept for loading conventional bombs in the B-52. Bombs were pre-loaded into so-called clips, as seen here, which were then towed to the bomber and hoisted and secured in the bomb bay. This method took less than a third of the time than the old method, of individually loading bombs onto the racks. Eighty-four Mk.82 500-pound bombs could be carried internally, and another twenty-four externally on multiple ejector racks. These modifications resulted in the "Big Belly" Stratofortresses, which increased the bomb load significantly. For example, whereas unmodified B-52Ds could carry only twenty-seven 500-pound bombs, all in the bomb bay, the Big-Belly planes could carry a total of 108 500-pound bombs internally and on wing racks. In the background is the tail of B-52D-80-BO serial number 56-0629, which was used in the Big Belly tests. *National Museum of the United States Air Force*

Two BUFFs, likely B-52Ds, are taxiing at U-Tapao Royal Thai Navy Airfield in May 1967. These bombers were part of a force of B-52s that were based at U-Tapao starting in April 1967; they were painted in two shades of green and one of tan on the upper surfaces, with black on the sides and undersides and a distinctive black vertical fin and rudder. Tail numbers, not visible in this photo, were painted in red.
National Archives

In another view taken at U-Tapao in May 1967, four BUFFs in Southeast Asia camouflage schemes are parked on the flightline. In the right foreground is a B-52D-60-BO. The tail number is indistinct, but it correlates to serial number 55-0095 or -0096. Serial number 55-0095 is known to have operated out of U-Tapao in 1967, while assigned to the 306th Bombardment Wing.
National Archives

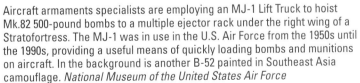

Aircraft armaments specialists are employing an MJ-1 Lift Truck to hoist Mk.82 500-pound bombs to a multiple ejector rack under the right wing of a Stratofortress. The MJ-1 was in use in the U.S. Air Force from the 1950s until the 1990s, providing a useful means of quickly loading bombs and munitions on aircraft. In the background is another B-52 painted in Southeast Asia camouflage. *National Museum of the United States Air Force*

Scores of M117 750-pound general-purpose bombs are lying on trailers at an unidentified airbase, awaiting loading into the B-52 Stratofortresses in the background. The M117 was an unguided, low-drag bomb that dated to the Korean War, and they were used extensively in the war in Vietnam. *National Archives*

Boeing B-52D-65-BO, serial number 55-0117, is parked inside a revetment at an unidentified base in the Western Pacific in 1967. The aircraft is prepared for a combat mission, with Mk.82 500-pound bombs mounted on the multiple ejector racks underneath the wings. Painted on the scoreboard on the side of the forward fuselage are scores of red bombs, apparently totaling 104, signifying bombing missions. *National Archives*

Aided by a drag chute, a B-52D is rolling to a stop on a runway at an airbase in the Western Pacific in 1967. Note the lowered Fowler flaps and the raised spoilers on the left wing. The number 625 is visible on the drop tank, signifying that this aircraft was B-52D-80-BO, serial number 56-0625. This BUFF crashed and was destroyed on March 31, 1972, while approaching McCoy Air Force Base, Florida, with the loss of all seven crewmen. *National Archives*

A B-52D prepares to take off at the beginning of the Strategic Air Command's eighteenth annual Giant Voice exercise at McCoy Air Force Base, Florida, on December 15, 1971. Giant Voice (later, Proud Shield) was the Strategic Command's bombing and navigation competition, conducted each year to help keep aircrews and ground personnel in a high state of proficiency and alertness. On the tail is the insignia of the Second Air Force: a yellow numeral "2" with wings to its rear, with a red border. *National Archives*

Although the original US Air Force captions of this and the following three photos identify the aircraft as B-52Gs, details such as the three-digit aircraft numbers two-panel radomes, the height of the vertical tail, and the lack of alternator fairings on the sides of the engine nacelles contradict this identification; these aircraft actually are B-52Ds. This photo and the following two depict B-52D-75-BO, serial number 56-0596. If the USAF captions, aside from the incorrect model designations, are to be credited, the scene of this photo was U-Tapao Airbase, Thailand, on April 8, 1975. Note the crew access door and ladder in the open position. *National Archives*

Boeing B-52D-75-BO, serial number 56-0596, is viewed from a slightly farther perspective in a revetment at U-Tapao on April 8, 1975. Red covers are secured to the engine inlets to keep out foreign objects and dust. A fire extinguisher on a hand truck is in the center foreground. *National Archives*

This final photo of B-52D-75-BO, serial number 56-0596, shows the entire aircraft, parked inside a revetment at U-Tapao on April 8, 1975. Metal revetments were intended to contain damages to parked aircraft in the event of an enemy attack on an airbase. *National Archives*

A B-52D Stratofortress painted in Southeast Asia camouflage flies low over U-Tapao Airbase on April 8, 1975. The landing gear is in the process of retracting; note the partially open main-gear doors under the fuselage belly. The tail number and the three-digit number on the nose are too indistinct to be read. *National Archives*

Boeing B-52D-75-BO, serial number 56-0604, flies at high altitude during a mission, presumably over Southeast Asia. The tail number, 0-60604, painted in red, is of the type introduced in the 1960s. The last three digits of the serial number are painted in white on the external fuel tank, which also has a white stripe along its side. This Stratofortress, which previously had served in the 99th Bombardment Wing under the nickname *East to Westover*, was based at Andersen Air Force Base, Guam, in late 1972, and is documented as having landed at U-Tapao air base in Thailand after a particularly intense combat mission on November 5, 1972, having survived a total of 333 external areas of damage. *National Archives*

During the 1970s, B-52s began to be equipped with GBU-15 smart bombs for antishipping warfare. On the right pylon of this B-52D are, front, a GBU-15 (Guided Bomb Unit 15) and, rear, a data-link pod, which enabled digital communications with the GBU-15s. Two more GBU-15s are on the left pylon. The GBU-15 is a Mk.84 general-purpose bomb to which has been fitted guidance and data-link equipment, television or infrared imaging gear, and control surfaces for steering it during its glide to the target. Once the GBU-15 was dropped, a weapons system operator in the aircraft guided the bomb by remote control to the target. *National Archives*

B-52D Serial Numbers

55-0049/0051	Boeing B-52D-1-BW Stratofortress
55-0052/0054	Boeing B-52D-5-BW Stratofortress
55-0055/0060	Boeing B-52D-10-BW Stratofortress
55-0061/0064	Boeing B-52D-15-BW Stratofortress
55-0065/0067	Boeing B-52D-20-BW Stratofortress
55-0068/0088	Boeing B-52D-55-BO Stratofortress
55-0089/0104	Boeing B-52D-60-BO Stratofortress
55-0105/0117	Boeing B-52D-65-BO Stratofortress
55-0673/0675	Boeing B-52D-20-BW Stratofortress
55-0676/0680	Boeing B-52D-25-BW Stratofortress
56-0580/0590	Boeing B-52D-70-BO Stratofortress
56-0591/0610	Boeing B-52D-75-BO Stratofortress
56-0611/0630	Boeing B-52D-80-BO Stratofortress
56-0657/0668	Boeing B-52D-30-BW Stratofortress
56-0669/0680	Boeing B-52D-35-BW Stratofortress
56-0681/0698	Boeing B-52D-40-BW Stratofortress

On December 18, 1972, the first night of Operation Linebacker II, B-52D-75-BO, serial number 56-0608, with the 9th Bombardment Wing, was shot down during a strike on Hanoi. Part of the BUFF crashed into Huu Tiep Lake, in the Ba Dinh district of Hanoi, as seen here. That lake is now called B-52 Lake, and the remains of the B-52D have been collected and are now on display at the Museum of Victory Over B-52, in Hanoi. *Department of Defense*

CHAPTER 7
B-52E

The B-52E was designed and built from the first as a low-level bomber. To enable the aircraft to operate in the rigorous low-level environment, the B-52E was equipped with the IBM AN/ASQ-38 bombing and navigation system. The B-52E was virtually identical to the B-52D in exterior appearance. Fifty-eight B-52Es were completed at Boeing's Wichita, Kansas, plant, while forty-two were built at Seattle, for a total of one hundred B-52Es. This photo shows the first plane of that model, B-52E-1-BO, serial number 56-0631, flying very low over a coastline in the Pacific Northwest. *Department of Defense*

The B-52E was born from a shift in SAC strategy. The Strategic Air Command was becoming increasingly wary of advances in Soviet surface to air missile capability. Not only were the missile technologies improving, but so was the network, which left virtually no point on the Soviet border without a nearby missile battery. This led to the decision to abandon plans for high-level nuclear bomb attack in favor of a low-level attack strategy, attacking from levels as low as 500 feet.

In order to accommodate the new attack plan, more sophisticated avionics were required. At the heart of the B-52E was the IBM AN/ASQ-38 bombing and navigation system. This automated analog system was comprised of four parts:

- MD-1 automatic astrocompass
- AN/AJA-1 or AN/AJN-8 true heading computer system
- AN/APN-89A Doppler radar
- AN/ASB-9A or AN/ASB-16 bombing navigation system

The AN/APN-89A Doppler radar provided ground speed and drift information to the bombing navigation system. Latitude/longitude information was fed to the bombing navigation system by the true heading computer and the astrocompass.

While the ASQ-38 bombing/navigation system was state of the art at the time, and was factory installed in the B-52E and all later models, it was not initially as accurate as had been anticipated, and was also difficult to maintain. In the late 1950s, a program known as Jolly Well began to improve the performance of the ASQ-38 system throughout the B-52 fleet. This program was not complete until 1964.

Four contracts, providing funding in fiscal years 1956 and 1957, covered the production of the one hundred B-52Es. They were:

1. AF33(600)-31155 signed August 10, 1955, for fourteen Wichita-built B-52Es, serial numbers 56-0699 thru 56-0712.
2. AF33(600)-31267 signed October 26, 1955, included twenty-six Seattle-built B-52Es serial numbers 56-0631 thru 56-0656 as well as some B-52Ds.
3. AF33(600)-32863 signed July 2, 1956, was for sixteen Seattle-built B-52Es, serial numbers 57-0014 to 57-0029.
4. AF33(600)-32864, signed July 2, 1956, included forty-four Wichita-built B-52Es, serial numbers 57-0095 thru 57-0138.

The first B-52E, Seattle-built 56-0631, made its first flight on October 3, 1957, and exactly two weeks later Wichita's first B-52E took off on its maiden flight. The final B-52E was accepted by the Air Force in June 1958. The B-52E became operational in the SAC inventory in December 1957, with the 6th Bomb Wing at Walker Air Force Base. The B-52E was withdrawn from operational service in 1970, when the aircraft of the 22nd and 96th Bomb Wings were retired to the boneyard at Davis-Monthan Air Force Base.

Boeing B-52E-1-BO, serial number 56-0631, flies at low altitude, outbound to sea from a coastline. The E model Stratofortresses carried the same huge 3,000-gallon auxiliary fuel tanks as the C and D models. This aircraft made its first flight on October 3, 1957. *National Museum of the United States Air Force*

The landing gear and the Fowler flaps have been lowered on B-52E, serial number 56-0631. Engines for the B-52Es were Pratt & Whitney J57-P-29WA or -19W turbojets. *National Museum of the United States Air Force*

Landing gear retracted, the first B-52E flies low over Boeing Field, in Seattle. According to at least one source, this photo shows the plane upon takeoff during its first flight, on October 3, 1957. *National Museum of the United States Air Force*

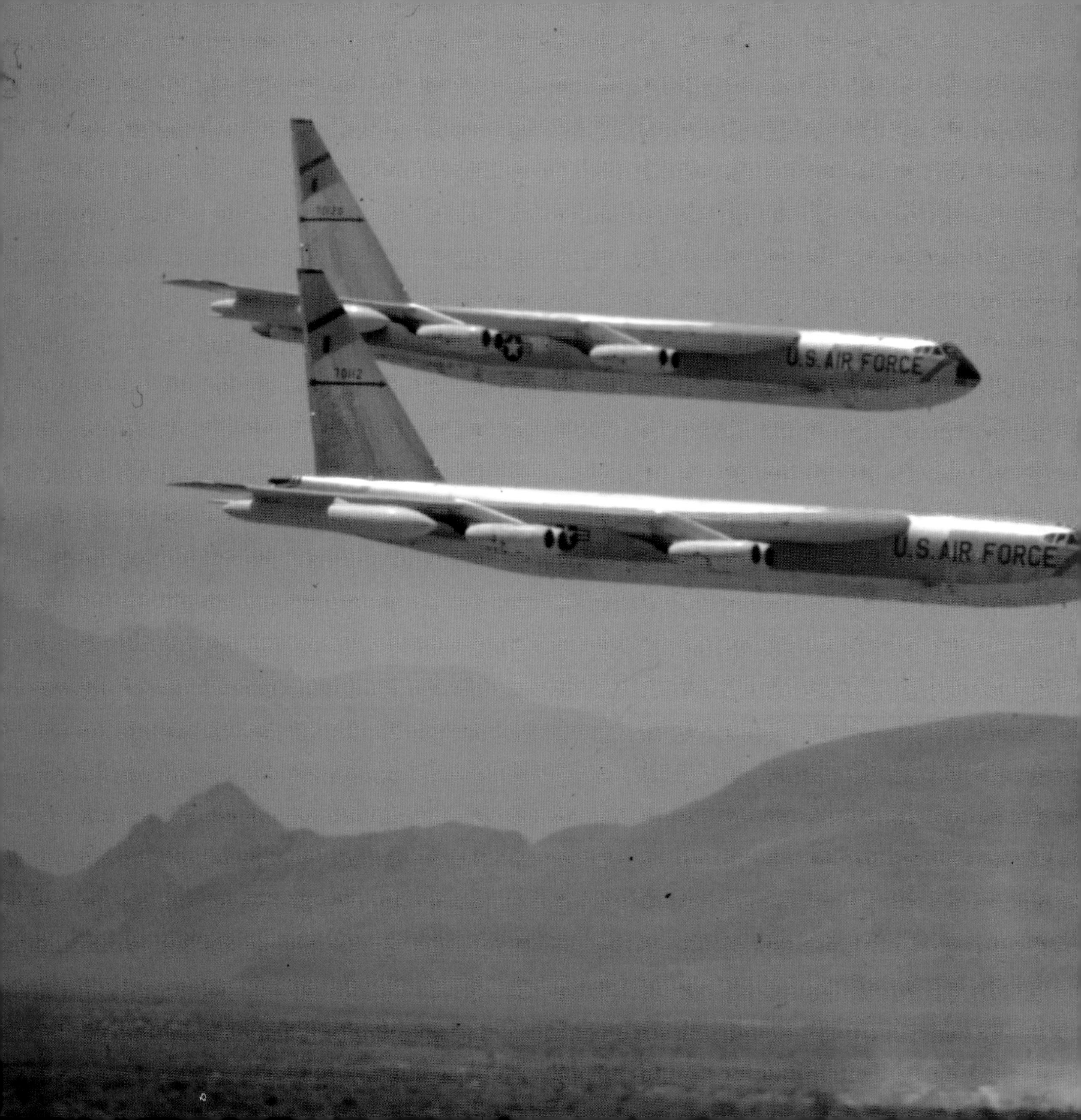
U.S. AIR FORCE
70112
U.S. AIR FORCE

Two B-52E-55-BWs fly in close formation at very low altitude in a demonstration held during the World Congress of Flight near Las Vegas, Nevada, in April 1959. The closer aircraft is serial number 57-0112, while the other one appears to be 57-0120 (the last digit is indistinct and may possibly have been a 6 or an 8). *National Archives*

Spectators at an airshow line up to view Wichita-built B-52E-45-BW, serial number 56-0701, which is painted in the so-called SIOP (Single Integrated Operational Plan) camouflage scheme, similar to the Southeast Asia camouflage, except, instead of black on the vertical tail, fuselage sides, and the undersides of the aircraft, there was white only on the undersides. On the pylon under the left wing is an AGM-28 (GAM-77 up to June 1963) Hound Dog air-launched cruise missile. The Hound Dog, which entered service in 1960 and served until the mid-1970s, was powered by a Pratt & Whitney J-52-P3 turbojet engine. With an operational range of 785 miles, it carried a W28 Class D thermonuclear warhead. *National Museum of the United States Air Force*

A GAM-77/AGM-28 Hound Dog cruise missile installation on a B-52 is viewed from the left front. Two of these missiles would be carried on the B-52, one under each wing. The Hound Dog was guided by an inertial navigation system; a star tracker in the pylon made navigational corrections while the missile was being carried to its launch point. The rated speed was Mach 2.1. On this Hound Dog, the SAC sash and shield are marked on the engine nacelle. *National Museum of the United States Air Force*

Throughout its entire career, the second B-52E, serial number 56-0632, was used to test prototype subsystems, including engines and landing gears. Subsequently, this Stratofortress was modified to conduct certain development projects, such as systems for suppressing buffeting at low altitudes, receiving the new designation NB-52E. A long probe was installed on the nose, fins were mounted on the sides and bottom of the forward fuselage, and a large amount of test instruments was loaded into the fuselage. The number of control surfaces on the wings was doubled, and these surfaces received electronic actuators. To support its research mission, the interior of the NB-52E was loaded with measuring instrumentation. The NB-52E was retired from service in June 1974. As seen in this photo, the NB-52E had bulges on the left sides of the engine nacelles to accommodate new alternators; these bulges were similar to those that would become standard starting with the B-52F. *National Museum of the United States Air Force*

Boeing B-52E-55-BW, serial number 57-0119, was redesignated JB-52E and bailed to General Electric for use in flight-testing the GE XTF-39 turbofan engine for the Lockheed C-5A Galaxy program. One of these engines was installed in place of the twin inboard J57 turbojet engines on the right wing, as seen in this photograph. The XTF39 engines were rated at 40,000 pounds thrust. *National Archives*

The JB-52E with the GE XTF-39 turbofan engine on the inboard position under the right wing is viewed from below during a test flight out of Edwards Air Force Base. The last four digits of the serial number, 0119, were painted on each side of the nose, between the upper and the lower radomes.
National Archives

The Boeing JB-52E is seen from the lower right during a test flight. The first test flight of the JB-52E with the XTF-39 engine was on June 9, 1967. That test flight and the second one, seven days later, met all of the objectives of the tests. The engine, which measured 8.5 feet in diameter at the intake, and was twenty-seven feet long, developed thrust equal to that of four J57 turbojet engines. *National Archives*

CHAPTER 8
B-52F

Design work on the sixth production model of the Stratofortress, the B-52F, commenced in May 1954, with production beginning in January 1958. The first flight was on May 6, 1958. Eighty-nine B-52Fs were completed: forty-five in Wichita and forty-four in Seattle. The B-52F was equipped with engine-powered alternators, which resulted in a prominent bulge on the lower left of each twin-engine nacelle. At the front of each of these bulges was a cooling-air inlet. The other main distinguishing feature of the B-52F compared with the B-52E was the installation of either the Pratt & Whitney J57-P-43W, J57-P-43WA, or J57-P-43WB water-injected engines, rated at 13,750 pounds static thrust with water injection and 11,200 pounds without water injection. Seen here in a 1967 photo is a long row of B-52Fs armed with AGM-28 Hound Dog missiles. The first plane is B-52F-70-BW, serial number 57-0176, with B-52F-65-BW, 57-0141, next in line. *National Archives*

Introduction of the B-52F brought with it several improvements to the Stratofortress design. The F model was powered by the J57-P-43W, -P-43WA, or P-43WB turbojet engines with water injection. These engines developed 13,750 pounds of static thrust each, and to accommodate the increased power output, more than 1,000 structural changes had to be made to the airframe. Another area of significant improvement was the alternators' supply of electrical power to the aircraft. The previously used wind turbine-powered units were abandoned in favor of new alternators driven mechanically off the left-hand engine in each pod. The previous units had been prone to bearing failures initially, and later turbine blade failure. The new units eliminated these trouble areas, but are externally distinguishable by the noticeable bulge on the lower left-hand side of the pod.

Consistent with SAC's new low-level attack strategy, long-range air-to-surface "cruise" missiles were developed, and the B-52 was to be the designated carrier aircraft for these weapons. The intended missile was the Skybolt, then under development, and intended to be carried by the B-52G. Until the Skybolt entered production, however, an alternate in the form of the B-77, later redesignated AGM-28 Hound Dog, would be carried, and the B-52F modified to accommodate it. Built by North American Aviation, the Hound Dog was an air-launched, supersonic, turbojet-propelled missile that could carry a W28 nuclear warhead, with a range of 785 miles. Some examples of earlier B-52 models were modified to accommodate the Hound Dog as well.

The B-52Fs were built under two contracts. Contract AF33(600)-32863 signed July 2, 1956, covered Seattle-built B-52Fs with serial numbers 57-0030 thru 57-0073, as well as sixteen B-52Es. Contract AF33(600)-38264, also dated July 2, 1956, covered forty-four B-52Es and forty-five B-52Fs, to be built at Wichita. The serial numbers of these B-52Fs were 57-0139 through 57-0183.

The first B-52F, Seattle-built 57-0030, took to the air for the first time on May 6, 1958, with the first Wichita-built B-52F lifting off the runway eight days later. The forty-five B-52Fs built in Seattle would be the last Stratofortresses built in Boeing's hometown. All subsequent B-52 production would be in Kansas.

B-52F deliveries began in June 1958, starting with 93rd Bomb Wing aircraft. In June of 1964, project South Bay was approved, directing the modification of twenty-eight B-52Fs. This project, with the objective of increasing the conventional warfare capability of the B-52F, allowed twenty-four 750-pound bombs to be carried externally on the Hound Dog pylons. This effectively doubled the B-52F's conventional bomb load to 38,250 pounds. The acceleration of the Vietnam War prompted Secretary of Defense Robert MacNamara to request that forty-six other B-52Fs be similarly modified under a program known as Sun Bath.

The B-52F was the first Stratofortress to take part in combat, when thirty aircraft from the 7th and 320th Bomb Wings were sent to bomb suspected Viet Cong positions at Ben Cat, forty miles north of Saigon. This June 18, 1965 attack was the first of

Seattle-built B-52F-105-BO, serial number 57-0039, is taxiing at Castle Air Force Base, California, in October 1959. The Seattle B-52Fs were produced in three production blocks, numbered 100, 105 (the plane shown here was part of that block), and 110. The Wichita production-block numbers for the B-52Fs were 65 and 70. *National Archives*

This photograph of the lower part of the tail of a B-52F provides an excellent study of part of the tail turret and other features. The black object to the immediate rear of the horizontal stabilizer is the right-side antenna for the APS-54 tail-warning radar system. The drag-chute box is in the lowered position below the fuselage. To the immediate rear of that box is the access door for the ammunition magazine for the tail guns. Forward of the drag-chute box is the exterior entry door for the tail gunner. Faintly visible below the entry door are three small, open access doors for the drag-chute apparatus. *National Museum of the United States Air Force*

A B-52F takes off on a bombing mission from Guam around mid-August 1965. A little more than a year before, under a project called South Bay, the Air Force had ordered eighteen B-52Fs to be modified to carry twenty-four 750-pound bombs on multiple ejector racks on the two-wing pylons, to nearly double the aircraft's bomb capacity, to 38,250 pounds. The loaded multiple ejector racks are visible under the wings of this Stratofortress. The bulges for the alternators also are discernible on the lower left quadrants of the engine nacelles. *National Museum of the United States Air Force*

the famed Arc Light raids and was flown from Andersen Air Base on Guam. The raid, which was panned by US press at the time, was a week later assessed by forces on the ground as having achieved almost total destruction of the target area. Unfortunately, two B-52Fs and their crews were lost in a mid-air collision on the

way to the target, the only two losses of B-52Fs recorded. By spring 1966, Big Belly B-52Ds had taken over the task of conventional bombing in Southeast Asia and the B-52Fs returned to the nuclear deterrent role. The B-52F was retired during 1978; it was the last of the "big tail" B-52s produced.

At Andersen Air Force Base, Guam, several 750-pound bombs and the wing of a B-52 are in the foreground in this view of *Lady Luck*, the first of the Fort Worth B-52Fs, serial number 57-0139. *Lady Luck* was serving with the 454th Bombardment Wing. These BUFFs are in natural metal finish, with black camouflage paint on the underside: a measure introduced around October 1965, for B-52s conducting bombing missions in Southeast Asia under Operation Arc Light. *National Museum of the United States Air Force*

The distinctive bulges with a round cooling inlet on the lower left quadrants of the engine nacelles are evident in this view of B-52F-100-BO, serial number 57-00034. Superimposed over the SAC sash below the cockpit canopy is the insignia of the 93rd Bombardment Wing, based at Castle Air Force Base, California: the first wing to be equipped with the B-52F. Multiple ejector racks loaded with bombs are on the wing pylons. *National Museum of the United States Air Force*

Casper the Friendly Ghost, B-52F-70-BW, serial number 57-0162, assigned to the 320th Bombardment Wing, is dropping a load of 750-pound bombs on enemy targets in Vietnam. Earlier, in 1964, while serving with the 2nd Bombardment Wing, this aircraft had been used to test conventional bombing systems in the B-52Fs and was one of the first Stratofortresses to be equipped with multiple ejector racks on the wing pylons. *National Museum of the United States Air Force*

CHAPTER 9
B-52G

The Boeing B-52G represented a number of departures from preceding models. It was the first model to be completely developed and produced at the Wichita plant. Two very noticeable changes were a much lower vertical fin and rudder assembly, and the omission of the ailerons, the work of which the spoilers on the wings now were to do. The tail gunner was moved out of the tail of the fuselage and was relocated in the forward fuselage, next to the ECM operator. The canopy in the tail turret was eliminated, and the relocated gunner operated the turret by remote control using the AN/ASG-15 fire-control system, which replaced the MD-9 fire-control system. The huge 3,000-gallon drop tanks were replaced by much smaller 700-gallon fixed auxiliary tanks. The two-piece radome was replaced by a single-piece unit. Many other changes and improvements were made to the B-52G. Seen here is B-52G-95-BW, serial number 58-0171, being refueled by Boeing KC-135A-BN Stratotanker, serial number 60-0320. *National Museum of the United States Air Force*

In 1955, the Air Force issued General Operational Requirement No.38, which called for an all-new bomber having the load-carrying and range capabilities of the B-52, as well as the supersonic capabilities of the B-58 Hustler. It was recognized that the fielding of this next generation bomber would take years, and thus Boeing proposed an improved B-52 as an intermediate aircraft pending production of the supersonic heavy bomber. The XB-70 was the ultimate outgrowth of the supersonic bomber program, and in fact was never placed in production.

The aircraft that Boeing proposed for interim use looked like the previously produced B-52s—and was in fact designated B-52G, but in reality was largely a new aircraft. While most of the avionics, as well as the engine systems of the B-52F were retained, the airframe itself was extensively redesigned.

Externally, this redesign showed up in the form of a tail rudder that was a whopping eight feet shorter than that used previously, and the reduction in size of the external wing tip fuel tanks from 3,000 gallons apiece to 700-gallons apiece. Slightly less visible was the elimination of the windowed tail gunner's compartment and deletion of the ailerons.

To make these changes possible was a myriad of hidden changes. The airframe structure was made of a new, stronger alloy, permitting it to be lighter. Integral fuel tanks in the wings replaced the bladders previously used, allowing the aircraft to hold 6,425 gallons more fuel than was possible previously—and thus the reduction in size of the external fuel tanks. The tail guns were now remotely operated, which permitted the gunner's position to be moved to the main crew compartment, dispensing with his lonely isolation at the rear of the aircraft.

More B-52Gs were built than any other Stratofortress variant, with 193 rolling off of Boeing's Wichita assembly line between October 1958 and February 1961. These aircraft were purchased on three contracts: AF33(600)-35992 finalized on May 15, 1958, purchased fifty-three aircraft serial numbers 57-6468 through 57-6520 with Fiscal Year 1957 funds.

Contract AF33(600)-36470 finalized May 15, 1958, added a further 101 examples to the inventory from Fiscal Year 1958 funds, and assigned serial numbers 58-158 through 58-258. The final thirty-nine B-52Gs were bought on April 28, 1959, contract AF33(600), and assigned serial numbers 59-2564 through 59-2602.

The new, improved, lighter structure of the B-52G, when combined with the new low-level flight patterns (with higher airframe stresses), meant that fatigue problems, especially in the wings, soon manifested themselves in the aircraft. As a result, a modification program was initiated, which ran from May 1961 into 1964, to correct this problem.

While a few B-52Gs were used in combat late in B-52 operations in the Vietnam War, it was Operation Desert Storm almost two decades later that saw the greatest combat use of the variant. On August 12, 1990, the first B-52G of the 4300th Bomb Wing (Provisional) landed at the massive US Navy base on the British Island of Diego Garcia. Over the next week it was joined by nineteen more B-52Gs. Despite the proximity of these aircraft to Iraq, once Operation Desert Storm was launched, the first Stratofortress action of the war was carried out by seven 596th Bomb Squadron B-52Gs flying from Barksdale Air Force Base, Louisiana. The grueling thirty-five-hour mission launched cruise missiles at high-priority targets, more than eighty-five percent of which were destroyed, and it was the longest combat mission ever flown. Officially known as Operation Senior Surprise, those who were involved dubbed the mission Secret Squirrel.

During the course of the war, additional B-52 strikes were flown from King 'Abd al-'Aziz International Airport in Saudi Arabia, Moron AB, Spain, and RAF Fairford, England. During the war, one B-52G, 59-2593, along with three crewmen, was lost due to an electrical failure.

The B-52G began to be retired in 1989, with the aircraft being hewn into large pieces so that Soviet satellites could verify the destruction for compliance with the Strategic Arms Limitation Treaty (SALT).

The B-52G introduced a new, one-piece radome instead of the two-piece radomes of previous models of Stratofortresses. It was hinged at the top and swung open for easy access to the radar components, as seen here. This B-52G, as well as the other surviving B-52Gs, was upgraded from 1972 to 1976, with the AN/ASQ-151 Electro-optical Viewing System (EVS), enabling the crew to better fly at very low altitude at night. The fairings underneath the nose aft of the radome housed the EVS, with the left fairing incorporating a Westinghouse AN/AVQ-22 low-light-level television camera, and the right fairing holding a Hughes AN/AAQ-6 forward-looking infrared (FLIR) sensor. *National Archives*

B-52G-95-BW, serial number 58-0182, appears here in markings it wore while serving with the 3246th Test Wing, Air Proving Command, at Eglin Air Force Base, Florida, testing electronic countermeasures (ECM) and radio altimeter systems in the mid-1960s. Photo-reference markings in the form of a black cross on a yellow square were on the forward fuselage and the aft fuselage. Orange bands were painted around the fuselage aft of the cockpit and to the front of the vertical tail. On a pylon between the engine nacelles under the left wing is an AN/ALE-25 ECM rocket pod. This pod carried twenty 2.5-inch folding-fin rockets filled with chaff, for interfering with the electronics of Soviet SAM antiaircraft missiles. *National Museum of the United States Air Force*

A North American AGM-28 Hound Dog missile is on a pylon under each wing of B-52G-100-BW, serial number 58-0210. The wings, canards, and vertical tail of the Hound Dogs were red, while the fuselage and engine nacelle were white. *National Museum of the United States Air Force*

The main landing gear on this Boeing B-52G are in the process of retracting as the aircraft takes off on a mission. It is carrying two North American AGM-28 Hound Dog missiles under the wings. The new, reduced-size auxiliary fuel tanks are noticeable. *National Museum of the United States Air Force*

Boeing B-52G-75-BW, serial number 57-6472, has just released a Hound Dog missile during a test firing. Colored bands are visible on the B-52G on the aft fuselage and the outer wing section, and a scalloped band is on the fuselage aft of the cockpit. A white cross on a black square, for photo-reference purposes, is partially visible above the trailing edge of the wing. *National Museum of the United States Air Force*

Four Douglas XGAM-87A Skybolt air-launched ballistic missiles are mounted under the wings of a B-52G in a photograph taken on January 11, 1961. The GAM-87, which was conceived as the primary offensive weapon of the new B-52H, was designed to allow the Stratofortress to launch the W59 thermonuclear weapon at Soviet targets at a safe stand-off distance; the Skybolt had an operational range of 1,150 miles. The Skybolt was powered by an Aerojet General two-stage solid-fuel rocket, and it weighed 11,000 pounds and measured thirty-eight feet, three inches in length and thirty-five inches in diameter. Test-firing of the Skybolt began in 1962, and because of a series of problems, the program was cancelled at the end of that year. *National Archives*

The sixth Boeing B-52G, serial number 57-6473, is carrying the XGAM-87A Skybolt ALBM aloft for the first time, on January 11, 1961. Two Skybolts are visible under the left wing. Drop-tests of these missiles were conducted in January 1961, with the less-than-satisfactory powered tests commencing in April 1962. *National Archives*

Undergoing maintenance at Travis Air Force Base, California, in 1970 is B-52G-85-BW, serial number 57-6487. The bomb-bay doors are open. The air scoop on the chin of each engine intake is an oil-cooler ram-air intake. In the right background is the tail of B-52G-130-BW, serial number 59-2591.
National Archives

Loring Moose Gooser is the nickname painted on the fuselage of B-52G-110-BW, serial number 58-0239, photographed at Loring Air Force Base, Maine; nose art of a charging moose is included. This aircraft has the AN/ASQ-151 Electro-optical Viewing System (EVS), which was installed on B-52Gs starting in 1972. The external manifestations of the EVS are the two fairings on the chin. Each fairing has a swiveling turret: the left turret contains a Westinghouse low-light-level television camera; the right turret contains a Hughes forward-looking infrared (FLIR) set. Both turrets are shown here traversed to the rear, to protect the instruments; the rears of these turrets have been painted to resemble bloodshot eyeballs. The fairing with the white front below the side windows of the cockpit housed three AN/ALQ-117 active ECM antennas. Finally, the fairing on the top of the radome houses an AN/ALT-28 ECM jammer antenna.
National Archives

Boeing B-52G-95-BW, serial number 58-0182, appears in an all-white paint job during a flight near Edwards Air Force Base, California, on June 4, 1975. This aircraft had been wearing that paint scheme since at least November 1974. The insignia of the Air Force Test Center, at Edwards Air Force Base, is visible on the forward fuselage. Later, after this plane was outfitted with the EVS upgrades, it was repainted in a camouflage scheme and received the nickname *What's Up Doc? National Archives*

In this undated photograph, B-52G-95-BW has now been equipped with the EVS, and visible modifications had been made to the tail of the fuselage. The bomber is in the process of releasing an AGM-86A air-launched cruise missile (ALCM), which is visible just below the open bomb-bay doors. The AGM-86 was introduced to the B-52G's offensive-weapons suite in the early 1980s as a means of improving the bomber's survivability, as the missiles could be fired at a range of over 1,500 miles from the target. Also, the B-52G could carry up to twenty ALCMs, in the bomb bay and on pylons, greatly reducing the enemy's ability to shoot down the missiles when launched en-masse. *National Archives*

Boeing B-52G Stratofortresses were adapted to carry the Boeing AGM-69A Short-Range Attack Missile (SRAM), which became the successor to the Hound Dog, beginning in October 1971, with the first SRAM-armed planes becoming operational with the 42nd Bombardment Wing in March 1972. The B-52Gs were able to carry up to twenty SRAMs: eight on a rotary launcher in the bomb bay and twelve on underwing pylons. The power plant of the SRAM was the Thiokol SR75LP1 rocket motor, and the missile had a maximum speed of Mach 2.5. The warhead contained a W69 nuclear warhead with a yield of 170 kilotons. Here, six SRAMs are loaded on the right pylon of B-52G-90-BW, serial number 57-6518. *National Museum of the United States Air Force*

During tests in 1979, six AGM-86B air-launched cruise missiles are mounted on the left pylon of a B-52G. These missiles had folding wings, tails, and engine inlets, which were opened upon launching. The AGM-86B employed a terrain contour-matching (TERCOM) guidance system to enable it to fly very low to the ground, to escape detection. At the time this photo was taken, the Air Force was conducting a competitive fly-off between the AGM-86 and the AGM-109 air-launched cruise missile. During these tests, from July 1979 to February 1980, the AGM-86 was selected, and further development of the AGM-109 ceased. *National Archives*

A B-52G carrying six AGM-109 ALCMs on each under-wing pylon is viewed from below during the competitive fly-offs to determine which ALCM, the AGM-86 or AGM-109, the Air Force would adopt. Although the Air Force would reject the AGM-109 for its use, the Navy would continue to develop and operate the ship-launched version, the BGM-109 Tomahawk, and the Air Force also developed and deployed the ground-launched BGM-109G Gryphon as an intermediate-range nuclear weapon for deployment in Europe. *National Archives*

The twelve AGM-109 ALCMs on the pylons of a B-52G are viewed from a fairly close perspective during the competitive fly-offs. When in the pre-launch configuration, these missiles had an appearance similar to a long torpedo. The number 0204 and the insignia of the Air Force Flight Test Center are on the fuselage of the B-52G, to the far right. *National Archives*

CHAPTER 10

B-52H

The final model of the Stratofortress was the B-52H. All 102 examples were constructed at Boeing's Wichita facility. A key difference between the H model and the G model was that the Pratt & Whitney J57 turbojet engines were replaced by that manufacturer's TF33-P3 turbofan engines. The inclusion of these new engines resulted in noticeably different engine nacelles, on which the alternator fairings introduced with the B-52G no longer were present. The front halves of the nacelles were larger in diameter than the rear halves, with the divisions between those halves being quite visible. In this undated photograph, B-52H-145-BW, serial number 60-0022, is carrying aloft a quartet of Douglas XGAM-87A Skybolt air-launched ballistic missiles during the short-lived testing of that missile system. The Skybolt was conceived as the primary offensive weapon of the B-52, but because of a series of mishaps during the testing of the missile, coupled with the new availability of submarine-launched ballistic missiles, the project was terminated in December 1962. *National Museum of the United States Air Force*

The final variant of the Stratofortress to be built was the B-52H, and today it remains the only type still in service. Production, which was undertaken only in Wichita, totaled 102 aircraft built on two contracts. The first, covering sixty-two aircraft, was contract AF33(600)-38778 and was signed on May 6, 1960. Those aircraft were assigned serial numbers 60-001 thru 60-0062. The final B-52 contract was AF33(600)-41961, which covered production of 61-0001 through 61-0040.

The B-52H differed from the B-52G most notably in the use of Pratt & Whitney TF33-P-3 turbofan engines, rather than the J57 turbojets, which resulted in a thirty percent increase in thrust as well as better fuel economy, with a corresponding increase in range. Additionally, the TF33 did away with the troublesome and laborious water injection system used by the J57.

When built, the rear armament of the B-52H was a GE M61A1 20 mm rotary cannon; however, in 1994, those guns began to be removed and the gunner eliminated from the crew.

While the B-52G flew combat in Vietnam and Desert Storm, the B-52H did not, remaining on nuclear alert. That changed, however, with Operation Enduring Freedom. Only a few days after the terrorist attacks on the World Trade Center, B-52s once again began staging at Diego Garcia, this time H-models. On October 7, 2001, these aircraft began combat operations, utilizing guided munitions to strike a variety of targets in Afghanistan.

B-52H utilization in Operation Iraqi Freedom began on March 21, 2003, with a "Shock and Awe" campaign by ten Stratofortresses carrying air-launched cruise missiles and JDAM weapons. In both Iraq and Afghanistan, the B-52s made wide use of precision munitions.

The B-52H, which has undergone numerous upgrades since the first flight of the type on July 20, 1960, appears to be slated to remain in service into the 2040s.

In a photograph taken before January 9, 1961, four XGAM-87A Skybolt missiles have been loaded on the pylons of a Boeing B-52H. For the GAM-87 installations, at the bottom of each pylon was a rack, in the shape of an inverted V, to hold two of the missiles. From this elevated position, the escape hatches for the tail gunner and the electronic warfare officer (EWO), between the cockpit and the wings, are particularly visible. *National Museum of the United States Air Force*

This image of a B-52H with XGAM-87A Skybolt missiles was taken at the Wichita plant and likely represents the same aircraft and occasion depicted in the preceding photograph. Although the Skybolt initially showed much promise as a strategic weapon, other weapons systems, including the submarine-based Polaris missile, rendered the Skybolt redundant, and President John F. Kennedy cancelled the program in December 1962. *National Archives*

A B-52H loaded with four XGAM-87A Skybolt missiles is parked at Boeing's Wichita factory on the occasion of the B-52H's first public appearance, on January 5, 1961. The Skybolt featured a two-stage solid-fuel rocket engine and its own, independent, guidance system. The nose of another Stratofortress is visible to the far right. *National Archives*

On the B-52H, the turret with four .50-caliber machine guns was replaced by one with a General Electric M61A1 Vulcan, a six-barreled, power-driven, 20 mm rotary cannon, similar in concept to the Gatling gun. Depending on the model, the M61 could fire up to 6,000 rounds per minute from a magazine containing 1,242 rounds of ammunition. The fire-control system was the Emerson AN/ASG-21. As was the case in the B-52G, the tail gunner was located in the main crew compartment, facing to the rear, next to the electronic warfare officer. *National Museum of the United States Air Force*

The airman standing next to the tail turret of a B-52H provides a sense of scale for the M61 Vulcan and its mount. Above the cannon are two radomes for rear search radars. The top antenna covered the right quadrant, while the lower antenna covered the left quadrant. *National Museum of the United States Air Force*

In an undated photograph, Boeing B-52H-155-BW, serial number 60-0051, cruises at high altitude, carrying AGM-28 Hound Dog missiles. The refueling-port doors on the fuselage deck aft of the cockpit are open, in preparation for an aerial refueling. The undersides of the bomber and a band around the rear fuselage were painted white.
National Archives

North American AGM-28 Hound Dog missiles are slung under a B-52H in another undated photograph. These missiles were never fired in anger, as they were used for the delivery of nuclear weapons only. The Hound Dogs were retired from service in 1975.
National Museum of the United States Air Force

Painted in SIOP camouflage, Boeing B-52H-165-BW, serial number 61-0008, is parked on a hardstand at Homestead Air Force Base, Florida, in May 1967. Over three decades later, this BUFF would gain some notice for its "We Remember Sept 11 01 /FDNY" nose art. *National Archives*

Boeing B-52H-165-BW, serial number 61-0008, is viewed from the left rear at Homestead Air Force Base, Florida, in May 1967. Worthy of notice is the small, low-visibility national insignia on the rear fuselage. The markings near the top of the vertical tail are "USAF" over the tail number, 10008. *National Archives*

On December 15, 1971, B-52H-135-BW, serial number 60-0006, takes off from McCoy Air Force Base, Florida, during the annual Strategic Air Command bombing and navigation competition. On the tail is emblazoned the symbol of the Second Air Force. Note the wavy demarkation between the upper camouflage colors and the white paint on the belly of the fuselage. *National Archives*

Boeing B-52H-165-BW, serial number 61-0101, from the 20th Bombardment Squadron, 2nd Bombardment Wing, based at Barksdale Air Force Base, Louisiana, is landing at RAF Fairford, UK. Five aircraft of this wing were staged to Fairford on October 11, 1998, to be prepared to support possible NATO air strikes against Serbian targets. This BUFF has the overall dark-gray camouflage scheme. The drag chute has been deployed from its compartment, which now was on top of the tail. *National Archives*

Heat-shimmer envelops a B-52H assigned to the 96th Bombardment Squadron, 2nd Bombardment Wing, from Barksdale Air Force Base, Louisiana, as it lands at Navy Support Facility (NFS) Diego Garcia, in the Indian Ocean, as part of the Second Air Expeditionary Group in support of Operation Southern Watch. This operation, which lasted from August 1992 to March 2003, was an effort to patrol and control the airspace over central and southern Iraq between the end of Operation Desert Storm and the 2003 invasion of Iraq. *National Archives*

Munitions handlers are unloading a B28 (originally, Mk.28) thermonuclear bomb from the bomb bay of a B-52H during Global Shield, an annual SAC readiness exercise, in 1984, at Ellsworth Air Force Base, South Dakota. The bomb is on an MHU-7/M bomb-lift trailer, equipped with castering wheels, to enable positioning the trailer and its load precisely under the bomb bay of the BUFF. To the upper left are the noses of several Boeing AGM-69 Short-Range Attack Missiles (SRAMs), on a rotary launcher in the rear of the bomb bay. *National Archives*

At an unidentified forward air base during Operation Iraqi Freedom, the third B-52H, serial number 60-0003, is ready for the next mission. This BUFF was assigned to the 40th Expeditionary Bomb Squadron (EBS). Its multiple-ejector racks are loaded with GBU-31s, which are Mk.83 1,000-pound general-purpose bombs fitted with Joint Direct Attack Munitions (JDAM) kits, to convert the "dumb" bombs to smart bombs. The GBU-31s are equipped with an integrated inertial guidance system linked to a GPS receiver, giving the bomb the capability of hitting moving targets or striking with great precision fixed targets. *National Archives*

Personnel are unloading AGM-69 SRAMs on a rotary launcher from a B-52H during Exercise Global Shield '84 at Ellsworth Air Force Base, South Carolina. The rotary launcher has a capacity of eight SRAMs, but only three are visible here. The launcher and SRAMs are on an MHU-7/M bomb-lift trailer. *National Archives*

US Air Force 1st Lt. Joseph Little, a navigator with the 40th Expeditionary Bomb Squadron (EBS), kneels in prayer next to his B-52H before departing on a combat mission over Iraq during Operation Iraqi Freedom, the 2003 invasion of Iraq. Note the two landing lights on the right front main landing gear and on the front edge of the left landing-gear door, to the upper right. *National Archives*

A Boeing B-52H Stratofortress is viewed through a zoom lens on a flightline on Diego Garcia, in the Indian Ocean, during Operation Enduring Freedom, the Global War on Terrorism between late 2001 and 2014. *National Archives*

Munitions handlers from the US Air Force's 28th Air Expeditionary Wing are placing Mk.82 500-pound bombs on an MJ-1B Munitions Loader during a nighttime arming of B-52H-155-BW, serial number 60-0049, during Operation Enduring Freedom. Faintly visible below the "0049" number on the fuselage is the outline of a map of Louisiana, with a small star marking this BUFF's home base, Barksdale Air Force Base. *National Archives*

During 2003, airmen serving with the 40th Expeditionary Civil Engineering Squadron are readying a B-52H for a combat mission at an undisclosed location in Southwest Asia. This was part of an effort billed as the largest bombing sorties by Coalition forces since the start of Operation Iraqi Freedom. GBU-31 1,000-pound Joint Direct Attack Munitions (JDAM) are loaded on the wing pylons. The JDAM weapons proved to be one of the most outstanding military innovations to be used in the wars in Iraq and Afghanistan. They were particularly effective as bunker-busters and in destroying cave complexes. *National Archives*

At an unidentified forward location, USAF maintenance personnel from Minot Air Force Base, North Dakota, are washing a B-52H from the 457th Air Expeditionary Group, in support of Operation Iraqi Freedom. The number 0060 on the fuselage identifies this BUFF as B-52H-160-BW, serial number 60-0060. Nacelle sections are resting on stands, for ease and thoroughness of cleaning. *National Archives*

A B-52H deployed from Barksdale Air Force Base, Louisiana, is about to land at Andersen Air Force Base, Guam, on April 2, 2003, in support of the current mission of the 7th Air Expeditionary Wing. This was toward the end of an amazing three-day period, in which 103 bomber sorties, involving B-52s and B-1 Lancers, were launched from Anderson Air Force Base, from March 30 to April 2. Faintly visible on the vertical tail is the code "LA." *National Archives*

A B-52H Stratofortress from Barksdale Air Force Base, Louisiana, is releasing live bombs and flares over Point Bravo, on the Nevada Test and Training Range, during a firepower demonstration to show off the BUFF's combat capabilities. The flares were fired in combat to divert heat-seeking or infrared-seeking missiles. The bombs are the Mk.82 AIR: a Mk.82 500-pound bomb converted to a high-drag bomb for low-level use by adding an inflatable air bag/parachute called a "ballute" (a combination of "balloon" and "parachute") to the tail, to act as a retarder. Most of the bombs in this view have the ballutes inflated. *National Archives*

A B-52H Stratofortress is making an approach to a runway at Barksdale Air Force Base, Louisiana, in preparation for making a touch-and-go landing. In the right background, another B-52H is about to take off. More B-52Hs are parked in the foreground, and an A-10 Thunderbolt II is in the right background. *Department of Defense*

With the EVS turrets framing the photograph in the upper foreground, Airman 1st Class Mitch Dexter, a 2nd Aircraft Maintenance Squadron aerospace maintenance journeyman at Barksdale Air Force Base, Louisiana, is making a preflight inspection of a B-52H during the Red Flag 12-4 exercise on July 17, 2012, at Nellis Air Force Base, Nevada. Red Flag is the US Air Force's principal advanced aerial combat training exercise, in which the air forces of many allied countries also have participated. *Department of Defense*

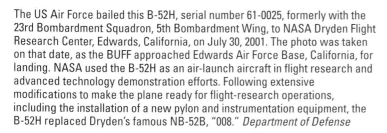

The US Air Force bailed this B-52H, serial number 61-0025, formerly with the 23rd Bombardment Squadron, 5th Bombardment Wing, to NASA Dryden Flight Research Center, Edwards, California, on July 30, 2001. The photo was taken on that date, as the BUFF approached Edwards Air Force Base, California, for landing. NASA used the B-52H as an air-launch aircraft in flight research and advanced technology demonstration efforts. Following extensive modifications to make the plane ready for flight-research operations, including the installation of a new pylon and instrumentation equipment, the B-52H replaced Dryden's famous NB-52B, "008." *Department of Defense*

A B-52H Stratofortress from the 23rd Expeditionary Bomb Squadron, based at Minot Air Force Base, North Dakota, is taking off from Andersen Air Force Base, Guam, on July 2, 2013. This aircraft was the ninth H-model Buff, serial number 60-0009. This plane formerly went under the nickname and nose art *Rolling Thunder II*, but by the time this photo was taken, it was operating with different nose art. *Department of Defense*

Personnel with the 2nd Maintenance Squadron are conducting a periodic inspection of B-52H-165-BW, serial number 61-0012, in a hangar at Barksdale Air Force Base, Louisiana, on November 24, 2014. During a periodic inspection, which is performed on all aircraft with more than 450 flight hours, access panels are removed, and engineers inspect the internal systems and mechanisms for defects. Faulty parts and components are replaced. Each inspection typically takes fourteen days to complete.
Department of Defense

A B-52H Stratofortress and its full complement of munitions are on display in front of the Base Operations Building at Minot Air Force Base, North Dakota, on September 21, 2015. The weaponry includes JDAMs, smart bombs, cruise missiles (including a rotary launcher with eight air-launched cruise missiles on a trailer in the center foreground), and two long trailers with Mk.82 500-pound bombs loaded on them. AGM-86 cruise missiles are loaded on the pylons. *Department of Defense*

Ghost Rider is the nickname of Boeing B-52H-165-BW, serial number 61-0007. This BUFF had been in long-term storage at Davis-Monthan Air Force Base, Arizona, when it was returned to active service to replace another damaged B-52. Ghost Rider arrived at Tinker Air Force Base, Oklahoma, in December 2015, where it spent the next nineteen months undergoing extensive repairs in programmed depot maintenance. This work was completed one hundred days ahead of schedule. Department of Defense

Chris Carson and Martin Harpster, aircraft mechanics with the 565th Aircraft Maintenance Squadron at Tinker Air Force Base, Oklahoma, are adjusting throttle-cable pulleys on the right wing of the B-52H named Ghost Rider during its extensive programmed depot maintenance preparatory to putting it back into active service. This was the first BUFF to ever be regenerated from long-term storage with the 309th Aerospace Maintenance and Regeneration Group at Davis-Monthan Air Force Base and returned to fully-operational flying status. Department of Defense

The engines are being started on several B-52Hs on the flightline at Minot Air Force Base, North Dakota, on October 30, 2016, during exercise Global Thunder 17. Global Thunder is a combination command-post and field-training exercise of US Strategic Command, to provide training from the planning of operations through execution at the tactical level, with a specific focus on cyber, space, missile-defense, and nuclear readiness. *Department of Defense*

Seen in a previous photo, B-52H-155-BW, serial number 60-0049, is being subjected to a bag-lift exercise at Barksdale Air Force Base, Louisiana, on February 16, 2017. Normally, a pneumatic lifting bag is used when raising an aircraft that has experienced a landing-gear failure, or when the nature of the terrain forbids using standard aircraft jacks. Here, personnel were practicing the pneumatic-lift procedure on a BUFF that had been damaged in a fire more than two years earlier. Air Force personnel had not attempted this method of raising a large aircraft since 1984. The pneumatic air bags are visible under the wing, and in the foreground are compressor carts, air hoses, and valve stands.
Department of Defense

Two aircrew members from the 23rd Bombardment Squadron, Minot Air Force Base, North Dakota, are preparing to exit through open hatches during egress training on February 22, 2017. They are seated in an egress simulator, which was fashioned from the nose section of a B-52G. *Department of Defense*

Using a bomb-lift truck, three munitions technicians from the 23rd Expeditionary Aircraft Maintenance Unit are loading a Joint Direct Attack Munition on the left multiple-ejector rack on B-52D-165-BW, serial number 61-0012, at an undisclosed location in Southwest Asia on June 15, 2017. The bomb appears to be a BLU-109/B JDAM, a guided, hardened-penetration "bunker buster." *Department of Defense*

Lightning is striking on the horizon beyond the seventh H-model BUFF, B-52H-135-BW, serial number 61-0007, on the flightline at Minot Air Force Base, North Dakota, on July 17, 2017. Crisp details are available of the nose and forward fuselage. Below the side windows of the cockpit canopy, a NACA air scoop is to the front of the teardrop-shaped fairing for active countermeasures equipment.
Department of Defense

The Big Stick, Boeing B-52H-170-BW, serial number 61-0020, has landed at RAF Fairford, UK, on September 14, 2017. The nickname and a cartoon of a caveman carrying a large club with a lightning bolt on it are painted on the exterior of the cockpit. For some time, RAF Fairford has served as a forward operating base for US Air Force bombers. While visiting RAF Fairford, *The Big Stick* was scheduled to conduct theater integration, flight training, and joint and allied training to improve bomber interoperability. The allied training was to include participation in Exercise Serpentex, a training exercise led by French Air Command. *Department of Defense*

The outrigger gear has cleared the runway as Boeing B-52H-170-BW, serial number 61-0018, takes off from Al Udeid Air Base, Qatar, on September 8, 2017. The aircraft is painted overall in a dark gray, and there are very few markings: just the tail code, AF 61 018, and the number 1018 on the forward fuselage. *Department of Defense*

Two B-52H Stratofortresses from the 2nd Bombardment Wing, based at Barksdale Air Force Base, Louisiana, are taxiing at RAF Fairford, UK, as they prepare to take off for the flight back home, on September 29, 2017. These BUFFs had been deployed to RAF Fairford for three weeks in support of bomber assurance and deterrence operations. The lead aircraft is B-52H-170-BW, serial number 60-0024. *Department of Defense*